Maximizing Opportunities Through External Relationships

Daniel T. Seymour, *Editor*
University of California, Los Angeles

NEW DIRECTIONS FOR HIGHER EDUCATION
MARTIN KRAMER, *Editor-in-Chief*
University of California, Berkeley

Number 68, Winter 1989

Paperback sourcebooks in
The Jossey-Bass Higher Education Series

Jossey-Bass Inc., Publishers
San Francisco • Oxford

Daniel T. Seymour (ed.).
Maximizing Opportunities Through External Relationships.
New Directions for Higher Education, no. 68.
Volume XVII, number 4.
San Francisco: Jossey-Bass, 1989.

New Directions for Higher Education
Martin Kramer, *Editor-in-Chief*

Copyright © 1989 by Jossey-Bass Inc., Publishers

Copyright under International, Pan American, and Universal Copyright Conventions. All rights reserved. No part of this issue may be reproduced in any form—except for brief quotation (not to exceed 500 words) in a review or professional work—without permission in writing from the publishers.

New Directions for Higher Education is published quarterly by Jossey-Bass Inc., Publishers (publication number USPS 990-880). *New Directions* is numbered sequentially—please order extra copies by sequential number. The volume and issue numbers above are included for the convenience of libraries. Second-class postage paid at San Francisco, California, and at additional mailing offices. POSTMASTER: Send address changes to Jossey-Bass Inc., Publishers, 350 Sansome Street, San Francisco, California 94104.

Editorial correspondence should be sent to the Editor-in-Chief, Martin Kramer, 2807 Shasta Road, Berkeley, California 94708.

Library of Congress Catalog Card Number LC 85-644752

International Standard Serial Number ISSN 0271-0560

International Standard Book Number ISBN 1-55542-847-9

Cover art by WILLI BAUM

Manufactured in the United States of America. Printed on acid-free paper.

Ordering Information

The paperback sourcebooks listed below are published quarterly and can be ordered either by subscription or single copy.

Subscriptions cost $56.00 per year for institutions, agencies, and libraries. Individuals can subscribe at the special rate of $42.00 per year *if payment is by personal check*. (Note that the full rate of $56.00 applies if payment is by institutional check, even if the subscription is designated for an individual.) Standing orders are accepted.

Single copies are available at $12.95 when payment accompanies order. (California, New Jersey, New York, and Washington, D.C., residents please include appropriate sales tax.) For billed orders, cost per copy is $12.95 plus postage and handling.

Substantial discounts are offered to organizations and individuals wishing to purchase bulk quantities of Jossey-Bass sourcebooks. Please inquire.

Please note that these prices are for the calendar year 1989 and are subject to change without notice. Also, some titles may be out of print and therefore not available for sale.

To ensure correct and prompt delivery, all orders must give either the *name of an individual* or an *official purchase order number*. Please submit your order as follows:

Subscriptions: specify series and year subscription is to begin.
Single Copies: specify sourcebook code (such as, HE1) and first two words of title.

Mail all orders to:
   Jossey-Bass Inc., Publishers
   350 Sansome Street
   San Francisco, California 94104

New Directions for Higher Education Series
Martin Kramer, *Editor-in-Chief*

HE1   *Facilitating Faculty Development*, Mervin Freedman
HE2   *Strategies for Budgeting*, George Kaludis
HE3   *Services for Students*, Joseph Katz

HE4	*Evaluating Learning and Teaching,* C. Robert Pace
HE5	*Encountering the Unionized University,* Jack H. Schuster
HE6	*Implementing Field Experience Education,* John Duley
HE7	*Avoiding Conflict in Faculty Personnel Practices,* Richard Peairs
HE8	*Improving Statewide Planning,* James L. Wattenbarger, Louis W. Bender
HE9	*Planning the Future of the Undergraduate College,* Donald G. Trites
HE10	*Individualizing Education by Learning Contracts,* Neal R. Berte
HE11	*Meeting Women's New Educational Needs,* Clare Rose
HE12	*Strategies for Significant Survival,* Clifford T. Stewart, Thomas R. Harvey
HE13	*Promoting Consumer Protection for Students,* Joan S. Stark
HE14	*Expanding Recurrent and Nonformal Education,* David Harman
HE15	*A Comprehensive Approach to Institutional Development,* William Bergquist, William Shoemaker
HE16	*Improving Educational Outcomes,* Oscar Lenning
HE17	*Renewing and Evaluating Teaching,* John A. Centra
HE18	*Redefining Service, Research, and Teaching,* Warren Bryan Martin
HE19	*Managing Turbulence and Change,* John D. Millett
HE20	*Increasing Basic Skills by Developmental Studies,* John E. Roueche
HE21	*Marketing Higher Education,* David W. Barton, Jr.
HE22	*Developing and Evaluating Administrative Leadership,* Charles F. Fisher
HE23	*Admitting and Assisting Students After Bakke,* Alexander W. Astin, Bruce Fuller, Kenneth C. Green
HE24	*Institutional Renewal Through the Improvement of Teaching,* Jerry G. Gaff
HE25	*Assuring Access for the Handicapped,* Martha Ross Redden
HE26	*Assessing Financial Health,* Carol Frances, Sharon L. Coldren
HE27	*Building Bridges to the Public,* Louis T. Benezet, Frances W. Magnusson
HE28	*Preparing for the New Decade,* Larry W. Jones, Franz A. Nowotny
HE29	*Educating Learners of All Ages,* Elinor Greenberg, Kathleen M. O'Donnell, William Bergquist
HE30	*Managing Facilities More Effectively,* Harvey H. Kaiser
HE31	*Rethinking College Responsibilities for Values,* Mary Louise McBee
HE32	*Resolving Conflict in Higher Education,* Jane E. McCarthy
HE33	*Professional Ethics in University Administration,* Ronald H. Stein, M. Carlota Baca
HE34	*New Approaches to Energy Conservation,* Sidney G. Tickton
HE35	*Management Science Applications to Academic Administration,* James A. Wilson
HE36	*Academic Leaders as Managers,* Robert H. Atwell, Madeleine F. Green
HE37	*Designing Academic Program Reviews,* Richard F. Wilson
HE38	*Successful Responses to Financial Difficulties,* Carol Frances
HE39	*Priorities for Academic Libraries,* Thomas J. Galvin, Beverly P. Lynch
HE40	*Meeting Student Aid Needs in a Period of Retrenchment,* Martin Kramer
HE41	*Issues in Faculty Personnel Policies,* Jon W. Fuller
HE42	*Management Techniques for Small and Specialized Institutions,* Andrew J. Falender, John C. Merson
HE43	*Meeting the New Demand for Standards,* Jonathan R. Warren
HE44	*The Expanding Role of Telecommunications in Higher Education,* Pamela J. Tate, Marilyn Kressel
HE45	*Women in Higher Education Administration,* Adrian Tinsley, Cynthia Secor, Sheila Kaplan

HE46 *Keeping Graduate Programs Responsive to National Needs,* Michael J. Pelczar, Jr., Lewis C. Solomon
HE47 *Leadership Roles of Chief Academic Officers,* David G. Brown
HE48 *Financial Incentives for Academic Quality,* John Folger
HE49 *Leadership and Institutional Renewal,* Ralph M. Davis
HE50 *Applying Corporate Management Strategies,* Roger J. Flecher
HE51 *Incentive for Faculty Vitality,* Roger G. Baldwin
HE52 *Making the Budget Process Work,* David J. Berg, Gerald M. Skogley
HE53 *Managing College Enrollments,* Don Hossler
HE54 *Institutional Revival: Case Histories,* Douglas W. Steeples
HE55 *Crisis Management in Higher Education,* Hal Hoverland, Pat McInturff, C. E. Tapie Rohm, Jr.
HE56 *Managing Programs for Learning Outside the Classroom,* Patricia Senn Breivik
HE57 *Creating Career Programs in a Liberal Arts Context,* Mary Ann F. Rehnke
HE58 *Financing Higher Education: Strategies After Tax Reform,* Richard E. Anderson, Joel W. Meyerson
HE59 *Student Outcomes Assessment: What Institutions Stand to Gain,* Diane F. Halpern
HE60 *Increasing Retention: Academic and Student Affairs Administrators in Partnership,* Martha McGinty Stodt, William M. Klepper
HE61 *Leaders on Leadership: The College Presidency,* James L. Fisher, Martha W. Tack
HE62 *Making Computers Work for Administrators,* Kenneth C. Green, Steven W. Gilbert
HE63 *Research Administration and Technology Transfer,* James T. Kenny
HE64 *Successful Strategic Planning: Case Studies,* Douglas W. Steeples
HE65 *The End of Mandatory Retirement: Effects on Higher Education,* Karen C. Holden, W. Lee Hansen
HE66 *Improving Undergraduate Education in Large Universities,* Carol H. Pazandak
HE67 *Achieving Assessment Goals Using Evaluation Techniques,* Peter J. Gray

Contents

Editor's Notes 1
Daniel T. Seymour

1. Boundaries in the New Higher Education Environment 5
Daniel T. Seymour

Institutions of higher education can be studied in terms of their boundaries—the psychological and physical lines of demarcation that separate them from other social institutions. Given this perspective, the spanning activities that are the points of intersection across organizational boundaries may form the basis for maximizing opportunities through external relationships.

2. Openness and Opportunity 25
Ernest A. Lynton

Increasing permeability of the boundaries of colleges and universities creates substantial opportunities for new and exciting relationships. But why are the boundaries fading? More important, how can we take advantage of these relationships and still protect the essence of academic life?

3. Managing the New Frontier Between Colleges and Companies 43
Lee Teitel

Institutions of higher education are being profoundly influenced by collaborations with business and industry. A number of leading-edge partnerships illustrate the organizational structures being developed by educational institutions to facilitate these interactions.

4. Colleges and State Government: Problems or Opportunities? 65
Robert J. Barak

Colleges and universities have accepted the notion that to take advantage of new opportunities they must adapt, but the nature and scope of change is an ongoing debate. Of specific concern is the locus of control associated with adaptation. The boundary between institutions and state higher education boards is one of the core interorganizational links that reflect institutional adaptation.

5. Interinstitutional Comparisons for Decision Making 79
Robert H. Glover, Michael R. Mills

Interinstitutional information provides the basis for establishing meaningful understanding of relative organizational strengths and weaknesses. Such data have become increasingly critical to colleges and universities as they struggle to create and maintain a distinctive position in a competitive environment.

6. Communication Across the Boundaries 93
Robert D. Gratz, Philip J. Salem

In order to respond to external opportunities, colleges and universities must do a better job of managing their communication efforts. Indeed, maximizing opportunities is largely a function of applying effective communication strategies across the full range of boundary-spanning activities.

Index 113

Editor's Notes

The signs are everywhere. State boards of higher education and state legislatures have redefined quality in terms of their own world. What are institutions of higher education doing to enhance the quality of life and economic development in their states? The *Chronicle of Higher Education* (March 22, 1989) reported the results of a survey that noted that three out of four deans said that the time they spent on external activities had increased in the past three years. A recent issue of *Educational Record* (Spring, 1988) was largely devoted to presidents and the media. As one article began (Wallisch, 1988), "Like it or not, college and university administrators increasingly are finding themselves in the media spotlight" (p. 14).

In decades, even centuries, gone by, the quality of a college or university was largely focused on a single dynamic—the interaction of professors and students in the classroom. Institutions of higher education were mere collections of artisans perfecting their craft. These craft enterprises had simple organizational structures with few administrators, and those administrators who did exist were expected first and foremost to protect the professors' autonomy, to "buffer" them from external forces. But the expectations of state governments, economic conditions, the Information Age, and a broad array of other social influences have brought about a new, more demanding environment, one in which the problems of protecting the institution have been balanced by the opportunities of creating connections and linkages and where coordination and cooperation in the pursuit of a broader institutional vision is the emerging dynamic. Like it or not, the spotlight is on us.

This sourcebook recognizes a new definition of colleges and universities as social institutions that are important fibers of a broad social fabric. More important, it goes beyond a discussion of the mutual interdependence of systems to include a hard look at the opportunities implicit in these new liaisons. That is not to say, however, that this sourcebook merely describes a loose collection of activities that a college or university could engage in. Instead, this volume has a strong conceptual framework, presented in the first chapter, which is then followed by a series of chapters that provide detailed descriptions of elements of that framework. The framework that I discuss in Chapter One is rooted in organizational theory and the notion of boundary spanning. With boundaries being the points of discontinuity and intersection between an organization and its environment, one aspect of the enduring viability of an organization is its capacity for managing such boundary activities as environmental scanning, linking, representation, and information processing and gatekeeping.

Ernest A. Lynton, in Chapter Two, provides a rich discourse on the reasons why our colleges and universities are in the process of transformation. The second chapter builds on the first by setting a historical context for the changes that are occurring in higher education. Lynton also calls for the strategic management of boundaries in today's environment and uses examples of collaboration in research and development, commercialization, and technology transfer to illustrate.

Chapter Three, by Lee Teitel, examines two forms of industry partnerships: contract training by community colleges, and research connections with universities. While Teitel shows examples of successful partnerships and their corresponding structures, he also enumerates the problems inherent in the lowering of organizational boundaries—specifically, blatant commercialization, a loss of autonomy, and increasing corporate influence.

Opportunities in the external relationships extend beyond the corporate world discussed by Lynton and Teitel. In Chapter Four, Robert J. Barak looks at the relationship between colleges and universities and state boards of higher education. Institutions of higher education have employed a series of overt strategies to protect their boundaries from the various types of state boards. But, as Barak points out, protectionism must be balanced against the positive benefits that come from broad coordination efforts.

Chapters Five and Six look at different aspects of external relations. Instead of expanding on how industry and governmental organizations interact with colleges and universities, these chapters concentrate on two specific boundary-spanning activities: information processing and communications. In Chapter Five, Robert H. Glover and Michael R. Mills explore the link between institutional effectiveness and environmental scanning. By creating a decision support system that enables interinstitutional comparisons, the authors show how boundary spanning, and its resulting information-generating processes, can help colleges and universities gain a better understanding of their competitive positions. Chapter Six, by Robert D. Gratz and Philip J. Salem, examines external relationships as a function of organizational communication. More specifically, this final chapter analyzes the boundary-spanning activities enumerated in the first chapter in terms of communications strategies.

The quality of colleges and universities used to be defined in terms of the quality of interaction in the classroom. One philosophy professor and a half-dozen students: that was enough. But the twentieth century has seen increased access to higher education, the breaking down of racial and economic barriers, the expanded role of public higher education, and the exponential growth of knowledge in the form of new academic disciplines. Quality needed to be controlled. Accrediting agencies came into existence, program-review practices were developed, and, more recently, assessment and evaluation systems have come into vogue. Within the academy, we have responded to the changing dynamics of the student-professor relationship; but as social institutions, our colleges and universities have not kept pace with a similar set of changes that have been occurring across institutional borders. We have passively watched many boundary activities succeed or fail on an individual basis, with little or no effective coordination or control. The opportunities that can be derived from external relationships are limitless—resources, power, goodwill—but they also can be dangerous to the integrity of the institution and, at times, a tremendous fiscal drain.

The college or university of tomorrow must be as effective at managing itself in the form of external opportunities as it is in managing its internal budgets, staffing, and classroom activities.

Daniel T. Seymour
Editor

References

Chronicle of Higher Education, March 22, 1989, p. A11.
Wallisch, B. "Twenty Seconds to Profundity." *Educational Record*, 1988, *69* (2), 14-17.

Daniel T. Seymour is visiting scholar in the Higher Education Research Institute, University of California, Los Angeles.

Administrators need to develop strategies that cross organizational boundaries in order to coalign their institutions' strengths with opportunities in the environment.

Boundaries in the New Higher Education Environment

Daniel T. Seymour

Perhaps one of the most enjoyable aspects of being a college or university administrator is the lack of routine. Each day is different. A president may spend his or her morning in a series of budget meetings, deliver a luncheon speech to the local chamber of commerce, review the plans for a new parking facility in the afternoon, and spend the evening at a rousing testimonial dinner for the state governor. Similarly, a dean may begin his or her morning in a spirited faculty meeting, have a "listening" lunch with a small group of students, and devote the remainder of the day to marching through the agenda of the school's annual advisory board meeting. The activities can span a wide spectrum of adjectives. Some are casual, others are formal; some are crucial, others are routine; some are risky, others are pure status quo. The following case illustrations also represent higher education activities. As we approach the last decade of the twentieth century, they represent the kinds of tasks, programs, and occurrences that our college and university administrators find themselves involved with on a daily basis.

In the last eight years, the University of California (UC) system of nine campuses has grown by 30 percent, to about 157,000 students. Planners expect another 40,000 in the next two decades. Around California, residents in UC communities have begun to complain that the universities often act arrogantly and secretly. There is frustration that cities and counties have little zoning control over the state-run campuses. The increasing tension is perhaps most evidenced in the seaside city of Santa Cruz, which includes most of the 9,100 students and 3,000 UC staff in its population of 49,000. In 1987, the city brought a lawsuit that challenged the environmental impact statement for the construction of a new residential college. The case was settled only after the university agreed to hold annual public meetings about growth. A 1988 initiative in the city and county of Santa Cruz urged state legislators to cut UC's budget if the university does not pay more attention to the effect of its expansion on water supplies, traffic patterns, and housing in the area.

The city alleges that increases in UC students and staff drive up off-campus rents, hurting elderly and low-income residents; UC leaders counter that housing inflation is caused as much by the Santa Cruz area's becoming a bedroom community for people with jobs in San Jose and the Silicon Valley. Complaints about UC traffic clogging Santa Cruz have prompted UC officials to propose a road that would link the school directly to nearby highways. That proposal faces opposition because it would run through property intended to be a park. Finally, UC growth has created the need for more water resources. While city officials debated the feasibility of a new reservoir, UC–Santa Cruz began to look for water under its own property, with promising results. The search, however, has produced its own problems. Downslope property owners fear that UC wells will dry up their ponds and streams.

Project Advance is a program of Syracuse University (SU) developed to facilitate and administer a cooperative arrangement between the university and high schools. It is currently the largest program in the United States to offer regular college courses for credit, taught in high schools by high school faculty. It serves over ninety high schools and approximately four thousand students in New York, Maine, Massachusetts, Michigan, and New Jersey with course offerings in biology, calculus, chemistry, computer engineering, economics, English, psychology, public affairs, religion, and sociology. Instructors selected to teach Project Advance courses hold adjunct professor status at SU. They also hold master's degrees or the equivalent in their speciality areas, have extensive teaching experience, and meet the approval of their high school principals and the appropriate SU departments. Before the program is implemented at a high school, SU faculty in each content area meet with teachers in an all-day orientation to review course design. Instructors then attend a summer workshop that lasts from one to four weeks. It is conducted by SU professors, who both supervise the high school courses and teach the same courses on the SU campus.

The primary mission of Project Advance is the same now as it was in 1973, when a pilot program was launched in six schools in the Syracuse area. It allows high school seniors to take regular Syracuse University courses in their own schools at low cost. It provides in-service training to high school instructors and a continuing forum for communication between educators from high school and university settings. Project Advance also conducts extensive ongoing research and evaluation as part of its effort to improve instruction.

What do these activities have in common? They reflect a new definition of colleges and universities as social institutions that go beyond a set of buildings or even a group of people. Such institutions or organizations are, as described by Etzioni (1983, p. 6), "part of the encompassing structure of the community." This conception of our colleges and universities is far removed from the classic vision of an ivory tower—an internally oriented, isolated community of scholars. Instead, it is a view that stresses the interdependence of organizations in an increasingly complex social system.

Ultimately, most organizations are open systems. They engage in continuing transactions with their environments, receiving *inputs* in the form of finances, raw materials, ideas, and people. A *transformation process* alters these inputs—assembling parts, processing information, treating patients—and the resulting *outputs* go back into the environment in the form of refrigerators, new data forms, or recovered patients. The high school students who proceed from Syracuse University's Project Advance into a college or university are transformed over a period of four years into learned young men and women ready to apply their acquired skills to jobs in their communities.

Perhaps the most distinguishing feature of an organization as a system is that it must have boundaries—lines of demarcation between one system and another. Thus, the boundary distinguishes members from nonmembers, protects the members of the system from extrasystemic influences, and regulates the flow of information, materials, and people into or out of the system. The UC–Santa Cruz situation, for example, illustrates the process of protecting the system from extrasystemic influences (in this case, the legitimate attempts of the community to exercise zoning control).

No longer can campus administrators passively observe the activities that occur on the boundaries of their institutions. They must manage them, just as they manage their budgets or their staffing. The remainder of this chapter describes the nature of boundaries, both within organizational theory and as they apply to higher education. The final section is devoted to a practical enumeration of those "boundary activities" that deserve administrators' attention.

Boundaries: The Limits of a System

Boundaries have been described as lines of demarcation between one system and another. This definition has tremendous validity for discussing biological systems. "Nature has neatly packaged people into skins, animals into hides, and allowed trees to enclose themselves with bark. It is easy to see where the unit is and where the environment is" (Pfeffer and Salancik 1978, p. 29). The demarcation of countries also presents a visible delineation of boundaries, with well-defined borders that include guards and customs officials who restrict the flow of people and goods across the boundaries. Other systems employ psychological separation through the use of distinctive symbols, such as uniforms (the United States Marine Corps), dress (the Amish) or insignias (the swastika). In addition to physical space and psychological differentiation, boundaries can also be defined operationally by the relative number of interactions among any set of elements. For example, the members of a repertory theater group form a system, since they interact with one another more frequently than with the audience. The relative number of interactions, therefore, can define the boundaries of a theater group, a business, a church, or a college or university. By defining boundaries in terms of relative number of interactions, we can easily see how different social systems are interdependent. A professor is a primary member of the college or university to which he or she belongs. The professor interacts frequently with students, staff, administrators, and other professors. But a professor is also a member of a specific discipline—computer science, philosophy, history. Such disciplines have their own associations, their own meetings, and their own journals. In fact, a professor often has more interactions with other professors in his or her own discipline at different institutions than with professors in different disciplines at his or her own institution.

While the concept of demarcation is appropriate for defining the physical boundaries of biological systems and many psychological boundaries as well, the boundaries of most social organizations are not easy to see with the eyes alone. Therefore, it is more functional to define organizational boundaries as points of both discontinuity and intersection with their environments. According to Miles (1980, p. 317), "An organization boundary, then, is a region in which elements of organizations and their environments come together and in which activities are performed of such a nature as to more effectively relate the organizations to the outside world." Theoretically, an individual should encounter more resistance and expend more energy in attempting to cross an organization's boundary (for example, rites of initiation) than in attempting to move around in its immediate vicinity, whether inside or outside the organization. This demarcation or discontinuity exists because the very existence of an organization depends on the regulation of its boundary. Our ubiquitous high school senior could probably describe in full detail the resistance and energy required to gain admission to an Ivy League school.

Another way to look at the interfaces of organizations is to define the properties of boundaries. Corwin (1987) has described several such properties.

First, boundaries fix membership; that is, persons are either members of an organization or they are not.

Second, the responsibilities that lie within the jurisdiction of an organization are distinguished from those over which it has no authority; together, these properties define the primary boundary of an organization. For example, a person becomes a student (member) of a college by meeting various entrance requirements and paying tuition. Professors (members) are authorized to make assignments and assign grades (responsibilities). Persons who are not enrolled are outside the organization's boundaries, and professors have no authority over them. It is just such a property of boundaries that is at the root of the UC-Santa Cruz problem. The residents of the community, while not members of the university, are being subjected to the by-products of university conditions—a diminished water supply, inflated housing rates, and congested highways. Their response is predictable: they attempt to gain a measure of authority or jurisdiction over university decisions.

Corwin also defines two dimensions of secondary boundaries: permeability and containment. *Permeability* refers to the ease with which nonmembers can obtain access to the organization. A Unitarian congregation has a very high degree of boundary permeability, while a monastery has a low degree of boundary permeability. *Containment* refers to the ability of the organization to control its members. Organizations must provide some internal regulation over the interactions of their members. A military service has a very high degree of internal regulation, while a political party has a low degree of internal regulation. Similarly, entrance requirements and tuition (barriers to entry) in this country's most exclusive colleges and universities (low permeability) necessarily translate into a tightly knit system with strong solidarity (high containment). A local community college, in contrast, has low barriers to entry—high permeability and low containment.

In contrast to the view that considers the properties of boundaries, another way of looking at organizations is to focus on the people who operate at the periphery or boundary of an organization. These individuals, described in the organizational theory literature as boundary spanners, function as exchange agents between the organization and the environment. They filter information, interpret information, and act as gatekeepers and change agents. While many individuals in an organization may engage in informal boundary spanning, there are a limited number of people whose job descriptions require ongoing boundary transactions. For example, a purchasing agent fills a formal boundary role, while a corporate accountant does not; a college career placement officer does, while a residence hall director does not. Corwin goes on to suggest that boundary spanners have three types of relations in their boundary transactions: as sources of influence, as sources of discretion, and as sources of tension.

A number of other researchers have written about formal boundary roles. Persons who are responsible for boundary-spanning roles must cope with environmental uncertainties and in so doing must exert influence. According to Thompson (1967), these individuals must use *influence* in protecting the organization's technical core, in processing information, in representing the organization to external groups, in procuring resources, and in marketing products and services. The incumbents of boundary roles must also exercise *discretion*. The discretion of boundary spanners is greatest when tasks are complicated, when the environment is heterogeneous and changing, and when the roles have not been routinized (Aldrich, 1979). Finally, boundary-role personnel are continually under pressure to make compromises with external norms. Consequently, they must deal with ambiguity and divided loyalty. This *tension* requires that boundary spanners have such personal traits as egalitarianism, trust, open-mindedness, tolerance for ambiguity, need for achievement, and a favorable view of human nature (Brown, 1966).

Incumbents of boundary roles link the organizational structure to environmental elements, whether buffeting, moderating, or influencing the environment. As such, the skills of an organization's boundary spanners are also directly related to the success of the organization. Aldrich and Herker (1977), in a detailed study of boundary-spanning roles and organizational structure, have proffered two hypotheses that link boundary management and broad organizational goals: "An organization's ability to adapt to environmental contingencies depends in part on the expertise of boundary role incumbents in selecting, transmitting, and interpreting information originating in the environment" (p. 219). They go on to say, "An organization's ability to cope with environmental constraints depends in part on the ability of boundary role incumbents to achieve a compromise between organizational policy and environmental constraints, to choose strategic moves to overcome constraints, or to create conditions in which the organization's autonomy is seldom challenged" (p. 221).

The relationship is clear. Organizations are open systems, with boundaries that provide the functional means of controlling inputs and outputs. The successful control of these inputs and outputs is in turn closely related to the enduring viability of organizations.

Managing Boundary Activities

Up to this point, our discussion has been descriptive, defining the nature of boundaries. But the fact is that college and university administrators need more than description when it comes to the boundaries of their institutions. Boundaries need to be strategically managed—actively and aggressively controlled. Managing strategically requires administrators to develop strategies to coalign their organization's strengths and the opportunities in the environment. Such management recognizes that the organization thrives by being open to inputs, but selectively: its continuity and stability need both boundary permeability and discrimination. The organization thrives by being able to find markets for its output. It thrives by avoiding being controlled and by adapting to new conditions. It thrives by generating goodwill and amassing resources to act as shock absorbers that buffer the inevitable environmental conflicts and jolts. The organization thrives to the extent that it manages its boundaries well.

To gain a greater degree of control over boundaries, college and university administrators must manage a specific set of boundary-spanning activities. These activities include *representing* the college or university to its external constituencies, *scanning* and *monitoring* environmental events that are potentially relevant to the college or university, *processing information* and *gatekeeping, transacting* with other organizations for the acquisition of inputs and the disposal of outputs, *linking* and *coordinating* activities between organizations, and *protecting* the college or university from environmental threats (Miles, 1980).

Representing. Representation can be defined as the presentation of information about an organization to its environment for the purpose of shaping the opinions and behaviors of other organizations, groups, and individuals. In higher education's not-too-distant past, representation consisted mainly of college or university presidents making speeches and writing editorials and books. Many institutions subscribed to the "no news is good news" adage when it came to their public personas. But the problems of today have resulted in some colleges and universities adopting another adage: "The best defense is a good offense." In the face of increasing tuitions, athletic scandals, concerns over quality, and endless task forces and blue-ribbon commissions, there has been a growing realization that colleges and universities need to do a better job of telling their stories.

Effective representation improves the legitimacy and integrity of the institution. It enables the college or university to establish a measure of goodwill and allows the institution to maintain a creditable image with its different constituencies. It has even been noted that the practitioners of this public relations exercise serve the public and the institution in at least three ways. First, when organizations stress the need for public approval, their conduct improves. Second, when organizations make points of view articulate in the public forum, the public interest is served. Third, when organizations use communication and mediation to replace misinformation with information and discord with rapport, a segmented society is brought closer together (Cutlip and Center, cited in Ferguson, 1984).

In terms of boundary management, there appear to be three distinct areas of representation that should be of concern to higher education administrators. First, who is doing the representing? Second, what kind of information presentation is being conducted? Third, how is the presentation of information being conducted?

Who Is Doing the Representing? It is important to realize that many people have never been on a college campus; others may have attended a college in a different state; still others may be alumni, but from four or five decades ago. The point is that relatively few people form an image of an institution via personal experience. Any person who is affiliated with the college or university is therefore an unofficial representative of the institution. For example, numbers of faculty members act as consultants to government and industry. In such cases, faculty members are boundary spanners engaged in representational activities. The professor *is* the university to all the people with whom he or she comes in contact during consultation.

In contrast to the unofficial representatives, a number of individuals take on a more official status. In addition to a president, most colleges and universities have directors of public affairs, directors of communications, or vice-presidents of institutional advancement. As an important aspect of their jobs, these individuals deal with the external environment. In addition to official and unofficial representatives, the modern higher education institution has consciously spawned a breed of quasi-representatives in the form of advisory board members. In a recent publication that reviewed the structure and purposes of college and university advisory committees, it was noted that one of the most important purposes for which advisory boards are established is public relations, "the systematic effort to portray the institution so as to elicit feelings of admiration and warmth; in other words, to build goodwill" (Cuninggim, 1985, p. 12).

What Kind of Information Presentation Is Being Conducted? In an open letter to the nation's college and university presidents, the CASE National Task Force on Higher Education and the Public Interest (1988) stated that the only way that public attitudes are changed is to show that positive initiatives are being taken on campus and that meaningful results are being achieved. In the checklist for action offered by the task force, the emphasis is on open and honest communication. For example, "Should institutional reforms be considered, and if so, in what areas—

access, quality, price/cost, economic development? How will these changes be implemented and communicated to internal and external publics?" (p. 13); "Where serious problems have occurred on campus, has the institution publicly admitted to them? Taken immediate steps to correct them? And communicated those actions to internal and external publics?" (p. 14).

One such area that has received some attention is accreditation. In effect, when colleges and universities award degrees, they certify the competence of their graduates. The accreditation process adds credibility to such claims of competence, but in the light of concerns over quality, it has been inevitable that the self-regulatory nature of our institutional assessment procedures—that is, accrediting agencies—should come under attack. In such an environment, it is reasonable to ask how the practice of enforcing total confidentiality of accreditation reports is related to public accountability. Huffman (1982, p. 44) concludes his discussion of the role of accreditation by stating, "Accrediting agencies must be in the forefront in moving institutions of higher education toward demonstrating more effectively the impact they have on students. Only then will educational integrity be protected."

How Is the Presentation of Information Being Conducted? A number of boundary-management devices have become increasingly popular in higher education. Some colleges and universities are sending their administrators to media-management seminars, using news releases to spread the word, and hiring media consultants who help place stories about the institutions. There has been increasing use of "official spokespersons" in an attempt to insulate the president from negative publicity, to ensure that a consistent and unified position is projected, and to funnel media inquiries through a central office. Various kinds of "expert lists" are being promoted by institutions as a means of helping the media to easily tap colleges or universities, "speaker lists" are circulated to civic and professional groups; "fact books," "status reports," and other corporate-type four-color annual reports are being used to inform certain constituencies about the activities of institutions.

In general, then, the representational aspect of boundary spanning is intended to create and manage the image of the institution to its outside constituencies—to create impressions that lead to the enhancement of the institution's integrity, power, and autonomy in its environment.

Scanning and Monitoring. An organization can use two different types of information-gathering activities to look beyond its boundaries: scanning and monitoring the environment. Scanning is primarily an organization's search for major discontinuities in the external environment that may present opportunities or constraints. In more visual terms, the process is one of looking for "blips on the horizon." Monitoring, in contrast, involves tracking environmental indicators that have been established as strategic contingencies. It involves greater focus and a more detailed examination of changes over time (Miles, 1980).

Both activities, however, are functions of uncertainty. Environmental uncertainty has long been recognized as a key variable in the explanation of organizational performance. According to Thompson (1967, p. 159), uncertainty "appears as the fundamental problem for complex organizations, and coping with uncertainty, as the essence of the administrative process." For Thompson, the environments of all organizations are situated simultaneously on a homogeneous-heterogeneous continuum and on a stable-shifting continuum. The more heterogeneous or diverse the environment, the greater the need for boundary spanning. As the environment becomes more dynamic, going from stable to shifting, it requires greater information to aid the adjustment process. Therefore, the organization must be able to adjust to uncertainties, which are inherent in dynamic and heterogeneous environments, through boundary spanning. One of Thompson's (1967, p. 72) propositions states the relationship: "When the range of task-environment variations is large to unpredictable, the responsible organization component must achieve the necessary adaptation by monitoring that environment and planning responses."

Other organizational researchers have studied the notion of proactive management of uncertainty, or the positioning of the firm to influence its environment. The term *prospectors* has been used (Jauch and Kraft, 1986, p. 780) to define those top managers who actively search for change and uncertainty. Such prospectors tend to be more proactive and innovative in more uncertain environments; they also tend to increase their scanning frequency in sectors of the environment thought to be more important and more uncertain.

Few would argue that higher education's environment has not become more heterogeneous (with various community groups, state legislators, and others taking more interest in campus activities) and more shifting (with fluctuating student aid and unstable demographics). At the same time, however, few would agree on the particulars of how a college or university can embrace a turbulent society. For example, scanning is a useful boundary-spanning activity that can reduce the probability that a college or university will be surprised by future events or trends, but scanning is supposed to be the organizational equivalent of a naval radar system—looking across a long horizon for any event that may pose a hazard (or opportunity) for the ship. In a college or a university, this simply stated task takes on difficult dimensions. What areas of the environment should be included or excluded? Who should be responsible for scanning? How is scanning integrated into decision making and planning? During the last decade, for example, such seemingly diverse events as world oil prices, insurance rates, and the demand for professional degrees have had dramatic impacts on colleges and universities. The most common approach to environmental scanning in higher education has been the appointment of a systematic reading group. The group, usually consisting of a broad range of administrators, professors, and staff members, reviews materials from such sources as *The Wall Street Journal, American Demographics,* and the campus newspaper. Abstracts of particularly relevant articles may be routed to a broader group of decision makers. Morrison, Renfro, and Boucher (1983) detail the more formal "white paper" approach: when an issue has been deemed worthy of further investigation, a "white paper" may be commissioned, and faculty experts may offer their skills in research and analysis. The resulting document is given considerable exposure at all levels of the institution.

Systematic monitoring, as a boundary-spanning activity, has received significantly more attention in higher education than the more broad-reaching scanning activity, probably because monitoring is focused on a particular issue, is generally assigned to a specific person, and often entails a quantitative data flow. For example, the admissions office may track SAT scores by high school, the academic affairs office may follow faculty salaries and academic programs at competitive institutions, the alumni office may regularly survey alumni satisfaction and dissatisfaction with campus facilities, the housing office may monitor off-campus rental rates, and the institutional research office may follow regional demographic patterns.

In contrast with other types of organizations, colleges and universities face a number of important constraints in their scanning and monitoring activities. Hearn and Heydinger (1985) enumerate eight such constraints:

1. The discipline-driven structure of higher education makes it extremely difficult to balance the environment of "organizational whole" with semiautonomous disciplinary environments.

2. The act of defining a college or university environment is made more difficult by the oft-cited vagueness and diffuseness of institutional goals.

3. The highly politicized nature of many colleges and universities makes the role of environmental scanner into a powerful gatekeeper.

4. The need for future-gazing is often quashed by the more restrained, rationalist culture of academic institutions.

5. The loose-coupling within most colleges and universities precludes the timely, organizationwide environmental responsiveness possible in other organizations.

6. The cultures and histories of higher education institutions can result in most environmental influences being resisted as challenges to the status quo.

7. The lack of staff in most colleges and universities can preclude many institutions from involving themselves in an admittedly time consuming exercise.

8. The dominant governance norm of participatory management conflicts with the demands of turbulent environments.

Processing Information and Gatekeeping. Boundary management implies, in addition to scanning and monitoring of the environment, that knowledge of the environment needs to be interpreted, translated, and filtered. It does not help to have a sixteen-cylinder, four-hundred-horsepower engine if it is not connected to the wheels. But that is precisely what happens in many environmental assessment exercises, with the result that information is not properly integrated into planning and decision making: a great deal of horsepower, but little motion.

Boundary activities require that the meaning of environmental information be *interpreted* in terms of the opportunities, constraints, and contingencies it poses for the organization. Perhaps the best way to understand such activities is to apply Milliken's (1987) taxonomy of environmental uncertainty to higher education. Milliken hypothesizes three types of environmental uncertainty: state, effect, and response. *State uncertainty* corresponds to the uncertainty that drives environmental scanning and monitoring, when college and university administrators perceive the environment to be unpredictable. *Effect uncertainty,* however, is related to administrators' ability to predict the impacts that environmental events will have on their institutions. Being able to predict a decline in the eighteen-year-old population, for example, does not mean that you know how it will affect your institution. Effect uncertainty involves misunderstanding of cause-and-effect relationships and places greater emphasis on the boundary spanner's ability to interpret information. This type of uncertainty can paralyze an organization as administrators argue about the significance of information and engage in avoidance behavior instead of moving toward the formulation of contingency plans.

Boundary activities also require that the implications of environmental information be *translated* into terms comprehensible to organizational planners and decision makers. *Response uncertainty* is associated with attempts to understand what responses are available to the organization and what the utility or value of each option may be. This type of uncertainty poses a threat to decision makers, given a lack of knowledge about response options and/or an inability to predict the likely consequences of a response. The problem, therefore, is not the lack of information about the environment beyond the organization's boundaries; rather, it is the inability to translate critical information into a range of strategic responses. Response uncertainty often results in mimicking behavior. If we have accurately forecast a decline in the eighteen-year-old population and determined that it may have a disastrous impact on our institution, what should we do about it? Without the ability to translate state-uncertainty information into institution-specific options, we will probably imitate the strategic responses of competitive institutions.

Finally, boundary management entails some degree of gatekeeping—that is, making choices about what to communicate to internal decision makers and when to do it. Since open systems are inherently capable of change, environmental uncertainty can be viewed as an antecedent condition. The information-transmittal process therefore seeks to balance the institution's need for both adaptability and stability. Boundary-spanning activity must entail the activity of change agents as the institution seeks to align internal resources with external opportunities and threats. For example, the dramatic increase in professional degrees sought by college freshmen has allowed many boundary spanners to raise and debate the issue of the nature and future of the liberal arts in higher education. Thus, gatekeepers in higher education have a dual role in managed change, both as facilitators and filters.

Transacting. The term *transactions,* in both corporate and higher education organizations, refers to the acquisition of inputs and the disposal of outputs. On the input boundary, for example, a corporation has a purchasing agent, while a college or university employs an admissions officer. On the output boundary, a corporation has salespeople, while an office of career planning and placement serves a similar function on a college campus. Some individuals and offices serve multiple functions. A research-grant office at a college or university works with professors to obtain research funding from the National Science Foundation, the National Endowment for the Arts, and so on. That office also aids in the administration of the grant while the research is being conducted and helps to deliver the output—a research report, a program, or a piece of equipment.

The necessary resources or inputs for any operation are not free. Educational institutions must fight for place and position when it comes to attracting students, faculty, and staff. They must compete for alumni contributions and foundation grants. Effective organizations require thorough understanding of the nature of the competition and of their own relative attractiveness or advantages. For example, in Rowse and Wing's (1982, p. 657) discussion of competitive structures in higher education they note that "because two colleges draw students from one or more of the same pools of potential students, they are in competition with one another. Competition exists even though the two colleges may not be consciously competing or even aware of the overlap in student interests."

Just as resources are not free, so is the securing of product markets for an organization's output not guaranteed. In terms of students, colleges and universities must work with prospective employers and other members of the external environment to prepare students more fully for productive employment. The point has been made by Bok (1986, p. 180): "In principle, those who hire university graduates could put pressure on colleges and professional schools by preferring applicants who have taken programs that closely correspond to employers' perceptions of what one needs to know to perform effectively." The same is also true of all forms of knowledge transfer. Basic research—its production, interpretation, and dissemination—should be part of the extension and outreach undertaken by our colleges and universities.

In addition to clear understanding of the nature of the competition in input-output transactions, there must also be greater incentives for cooperation. For example, the Project Advance program at Syracuse University is an illustration of what amounts to the cooperation of two organizations over one's output and the other's input. Such cooperation is also possible at the other end of the equation. In an attempt to increase the pool of minority engineers, the Westinghouse Educational Foundation contributes a substantial amount of funding for college scholarships. Such programs have had a significant impact on the number of minority graduates with technical degrees: the number of minority engineers has doubled in less than a decade (Gavert, 1983). Such transactional cooperation benefits the college (output) and the corporation (input).

Linking and Coordinating. Another boundary activity that requires management in higher education involves interorganizational connections. As the emphasis in organizational research has shifted from controlling internal activities to managing external constraints, an important option for increasing control over environmental uncertainties has been collaborative arrangements between organizations. The types of arrangements that have evolved in higher education are extremely broad and range from simple ad hoc agreements between two colleges to legally binding systems. Although the range of coordinating structures is far-reaching, Whetten (1981) has grouped such coordination efforts into three categories: mutual adjustment (the weakest form of coordination), corporate adjustment (the strongest), and an intermediate category that he has called "alliance."

In a mutual-adjustment arrangement, the organizations usually have a narrow set of common goals. Coordination is done by a few staff members, with no central administrative unit and minimal commitment of resources. The rules tend to be ad hoc; no sanctioning is conducted, and disagreements are resolved through individual influence. In higher education, these arrangements have proliferated in recent years. The chief academic officers or institutional researchers in a state may meet several times a year to share data and discuss problems of mutual concern; for example, consider the National Clearinghouse for Teacher Assistant Training, which was formed by forty-seven graduate institutions in 1986. The clearinghouse is designed to be an organized system of information sharing on materials related to the teaching-assistant function at colleges and universities. A more comprehensive example of interorganizational coordination is the Holmes Group. The participants are a self-selected group of teacher education deans from the prestigious research universities. A concern for teacher education prompted the more than ninety institutional representatives to publish a report (Holmes Group, 1986), which calls for an overhaul of teacher training programs and licensing and establishes new ways to evaluate prospective teachers.

Corporate coordination is a much more formal structuring. The units being coordinated are members of an encompassing system, with each unit performing in accordance with a central plan. A strong central administration establishes systemwide policies and evaluates their implementation. System authority is the primary form of power, and there are strong sanctions available for control purposes. Few developments in the last several decades have had more impact on higher education than the creation of statewide coordinating and governing boards. The acceleration in the development of state coordination paralleled the rapid growth of enrollments through the 1960s and 1970s. Today, every state has some type of state coordinating agency. While the agencies' powers vary greatly, the current trend toward accountability has resulted in a significant extension of the mandates of such boards. As Whetten (1981, p. 13) has noted, however, such linkages lead to an inevitable strain: "this approach is generally resisted by participating organizations and consequently an ongoing tension between allegiance and sovereignty is a hallmark of most corporate interorganizational systems." The recent debate in Maryland is an illustration. State officials had proposed significant increases in the power of the new Maryland Higher Education Commission to evaluate role, function, and mission for all public colleges and twenty-one private ones as well. A lobbying group was formed to fight off many of the proposals made by the state's governor. After an intense, headline-making debate, the colleges managed to escape many of the new oversight proposals.

The alliance structure lies between the corporate and the mutual-adjustment structures. It contains elements of both—the linkage of autonomous organizations, without the authority of a formal hierarchy. Such structures usually have coordinating councils and have some limited sanctions available to them. This broad category refers to a wide range of federations, councils, partnerships, and coalitions. One survey (El-Khawas, 1985) of corporate-college collaboration showed that in addition to advisory boards and corporate-supported scholarship programs, there is also growing activity in the areas of shared equipment, employee training programs, and joint research and degree programs. One such arrangement is the research consortium. For example, Stanford University's Center for Integrated Systems began with fourteen corporate sponsors and $10 million in funding. Another option is the development of long-term individual partnerships, such as those between Monsanto and Harvard and between Exxon and MIT. More elaborate relationships are currently being constructed. The Rhode Island Partnership for Science and Technology is a collaboration among the University of Rhode Island (URI), Brown University, the state government, and local industry. Research projects are proposed by corporate-college research teams and funded by industry and state government. An executive director leads a board that includes industry chief executives, the presidents of Brown and URI, and the governor of the state. Perhaps the most vocal advocates of these boundary-spanning alliances have commented on the "substantial opportunities for the entire range of universities to cooperate with industry as well as government and other external constituencies in ensuring the rapid transfer and absorption of innovation into all segments of the economy" (Lynton and Elman, 1987, p. 21).

Protecting. As a consequence of growing interdependence, organizations make more attempts to obtain some degree of control over one another's activities. Therefore, boundary spanning should entail a measure of self-defense. While overprotection will cause an organization to lose touch with its external environment, underprotection can create steady dilution of an institution's mission and social system. One of the many distinctive features of higher education is its tradition of autonomy and academic freedom. As Perkins (1973, p. 127) notes, "To paraphrase Emerson, a university is a kind of 'standing insurrection.' In a perverse way, its legitimacy is a function of its heresies."

There is a general belief that state legislatures, governors, and statewide boards of higher education have become a significant threat to such heretical or freethinking autonomy. Newman (1987), in a recent study of state/university relations, enumerates a long list of factors that cause intrusion. The list includes confusion over institutional missions, overlap of institutions and programs, a focus of boards and systems on administrative matters rather than on policy, the desire of bureaucracies at all levels to exercise power, patterns of funding and criticism that create counterproductive incentives for universities, and so on. Such issues as quality and accountability have stirred state bureaucracies, which, according to Newman, have a growing ability to be involved: staffs have grown five- and tenfold, and they are armed with greater expertise and sophisticated computer capabilities.

State-level conflict is of the greatest concern, but there are also other potential problem areas. For example, it has been suggested that the close relationship between industry and our colleges and universities will cause applied research to drive out basic research. Professors may also drift away from their own research and teaching, in favor of more lucrative consulting opportunities with corporations. The Monsanto-Harvard agreement, with its $23 million price tag, carries a different kind of vulnerability. It is conceivable that, under such pressure for commercially relevant results, institutions could gradually lose their independence and be coopted by industry special interests. According to Bok (1982, p. 21), "Many of the journalists who have commented on the rising interest in corporate research agreements have suggested that universities and their faculty members are making some sort of Faustian bargain that will ultimately place their research under the control of corporations hungering for profit."

Certainly, such incursions as those made by administrative-hungry boards are inappropriate and call for strong protective measures. Such potential incursions as those inherent in various research collaborations also require vigilance. But incursions prompted by confusion over an institution's mission can be seen as appropriate and are brought on by an administration's lack of focus and vision. Therefore, the management of conflicting environmental demands must contain a mixture of mechanisms to avoid compliance—that is, the means to forestall a loss of autonomy. According to Pfeffer and Salancik (1978), the most effective way of avoiding the constraints of external demands is to avoid the conditions that demand compliance in the first place. For example, one important precondition for controlling external demands is awareness of the nature of such demands. State colleges and universities have had continual problems with state legislatures over fiscal accountability. The lack of mutual agreement on this issue has resulted in increasing fiscal controls, generated by state budget officials. Other avoidance mechanisms include the following (for a thorough discussion of adaptation and avoidance strategies, see Pfeffer and Salancik, 1978, pp. 92–111):

1. *Controlling the definition of satisfaction:* The power to control one's own behavior is enhanced to the extent that external groups that make demands are not well equipped to determine whether they have been met. This "equivocality" approach has traditionally been higher education's first line of defense. External groups that have wanted to know what a college or university was doing have usually been subjected to recitations regarding the complexity of the institution and its mission.

2. *Playing one group off against another:* College and university presidents have had to use this approach to balance the demands of governing boards against faculty unions. The administration must make a judgment regarding the strength of the forces that attempt to constrain its decision making and act accordingly.

3. *Controlling information:* The inability of regulatory agencies to acquire information regarding the activities of the organizations they regulate is a prime source of frustration. Colleges and universities have followed in the footsteps of most other organizations by releasing favorable information and withholding unfavorable information.

4. *Avoiding resource dependence:* The organization must take action to avoid reliance on a single source of input. Corporations use multiple suppliers and inventories. Colleges and universities have similar stra-

tegies: developing multiple student markets, endowments, and slack resources.

The interconnectedness of colleges and universities with other organizations has created an environment in which conflicting demands are common. The protection of boundaries in such an environment is a prerequisite of withstanding unwanted influence.

Life at the Fulcrum

While the survival of a system depends on its ability to maintain a basic state of equilibrium, its development and prosperity often depend on its ability to modify itself. A college or university depends on an internal state of equilibrium by maintaining its existing balance of forces while at the same time struggling to respond to pressures for change according to environmental pressures. For institutions of higher education, the uncertainty and intensity of the environment has brought about a new concern: "Successful institutions will be those which are able to broaden their strategic vision and which ride the tides of change while not sacrificing those educational principles they deem important. To do so, it is essential to look beyond our traditional organizational boundaries for ideas and information" (Heydinger, 1984, p. 5).

The concept of boundaries and their management is crucial to higher education because previous control mechanisms have lost much of their effectiveness. Colleges and universities no longer live in splendid isolation. Traditional forms of autonomy, such as limited accountability and self-regulation, have been compromised. Admissions officers forage farther from the campus, local communities want to have a say in capital planning, legislatures want to know how well their money is being spent, and colleges and universities want to portray themselves as key investments in the future economic growth of their regions. The result has been a basic change in the fundamental role and function of the American college and university. Our institutions of higher education no longer have the luxury of solitary and extended debates over philosophical issues of the past. They now balance on the fulcrum of today's information-based society and are expected to take a leadership role in defining relationships and creating linkages with industry, and government. This linchpin role requires that institutions become more closely related to their surroundings, that they establish ties with multiple organizational sets, and that they coordinate and facilitate the flow of information between and among the organizations.

In reviewing the boundary activities described in this chapter, it is evident that there are a number of strong reasons why systems and boundaries (in the lexicon of organizational theorists) have become critical to campus administrators. First, administrators must be adaptive in a changing environment. This is a fundamental strategic concern. A college or university that cannot change, adopting new ways of meeting changing environmental conditions, is risking its very survival. As an organization's environment becomes increasingly heterogeneous and dynamic, there is greater need for adaptability. Second, administrators must be politic in an interdependent environment. College and university administrators are experiencing the constraints of various internal and external interest groups and are compelled to move among them, hoping to build viable compromises among powerful blocs. As a coordinate part of a larger system, the administrator who wants to satisfy the expectations of one group may have to violate the expectations of other groups. Third, administrators must be effective in a competitive environment. Colleges and universities compete for federal and state funding, alumni contributions, new professors and students, community goodwill, and so on. Organizations flourish to the extent that they are effective. Effective organizations, in turn, are those that have the ability to acquire and maintain resources (or inputs into their systems). Finally, administrators must be vigilant in an intrusive environment. The previously mentioned environmental conditions have resulted in a more open system, one in which the boundaries that define the organization are more permeable. As the number of transactions that take place across the organizational boundary increases, the organization becomes increasingly vulnerable to dilution of its institutional mission, and sovereignty may be steadily eroded.

These conditions represent both a unique opportunity and a distinct threat. If universities and colleges carefully manage their boundaries, a leadership role in society is theirs for the taking. But if they avoid that responsibility or neglect to protect the institutional core, some colleges and universities face an uncertain future in which other organizations are likely to challenge their legitimacy and integrity.

References

Aldrich, H. *Organizations and Environments.* Englewood Cliffs, N.J.: Prentice-Hall, 1979.
Aldrich, H., and Herker, D. "Boundary Spanning Roles and Organization Structure." *Academy of Management Review,* 1977, *2,* 217-229.
Bok, D. "Balancing Responsibility and Innovation." *Change,* 1982, *14,* 16-25.
Bok, D. *Higher Learning.* Cambridge, Mass.: Harvard University Press, 1986.
Brown, W. B. "Systems, Boundaries, and Information Flow." *Academy of Management Journal,* 1966, *9* (4), 318-328.
Corwin, R. G. *The Organization-Society Nexus.* New York: Greenwood Press, 1987.
Cuninggim, M. *Pros and Cons of Advisory Committees.* Washington, D.C.: Association of Governing Boards of Universities and Colleges, 1985.
El-Khawas, E. "Campuses Weld the Corporate Link." *Educational Record,* 1985, *66,* 37-39.

Etzioni, A. "The Triple Role of Institutions." *Educational Record*, 1983, *64*, 6–10.
Ferguson. M. A., and others. "The Relationship of Public Relations and Board-Level Boundary-Spanning Roles to Corporate Social Responsibility." Paper presented to the annual meeting of the Association for Education in Journalism and Mass Communications, Gainesville, Fla., Aug. 1984.
Gavert, R. V. "Business and Academe: An Emerging Partnership." *Change*, 1983, *15*, 23–28.
Hearn, J. C., and Heydinger, R. B. "Scanning the University's External Environment." *Journal of Higher Education*, 1985, *56* (4), 419–445.
Heydinger, R. B. "Using External Information in Planning." In M. Waggoner, R. L. Alfres, and M. W. Peterson (eds.), *Academic Renewal: Advancing Higher Education Toward the Nineties*. Ann Arbor: University of Michigan Press, 1984.
Holmes Group. *Tomorrow's Teachers*. East Lansing, Mich.: Holmes Group, 1986.
Huffman, J. "The Role of Accreditation in Preserving Educational Integrity." *Educational Record*, 1982, *63*, 41–44.
Jauch, L. R., and Kraft, K. L. "Strategic Management of Uncertainty." *Academy of Management Review*, 1986, *11* (4), 777–790.
Lynton, E. A., and Elman, S. E. *New Priorities for the University: Meeting Society's Needs for Applied Knowledge and Competent Individuals*. San Francisco: Jossey-Bass, 1987.
Miles, R. H. *Macro Organizational Behavior*. Glenview, Ill.: Scott, Foresman, 1980.
Milliken, F. J. "Three Types of Perceived Uncertainty About the Environment: State, Effect, and Response Uncertainty." *Academy of Management Review*, 1987, *12* (1), 133–143.
Morrison, J. L., Renfro, W. L., and Boucher, W. I. (eds.). *Applying Methods and Techniques of Futures Research*. New Directions for Institutional Research, no. 39. San Francisco: Jossey-Bass, 1983.
National Task Force on Higher Education and the Public Interest. *Special Advisory for College and University Presidents*. Washington, D.C.: Council for Advancement and Support of Education, 1988.
Newman, F. *Choosing Quality: Reducing Conflict Between the State and the University*. Denver, Colo.: Education Commission of the States, 1987.
Perkins, J. A. *The University as an Organization*. New York: McGraw-Hill, 1973.
Pfeffer, J., and Salancik, G. R. *The External Control of Organizations*. New York: Harper & Row, 1978.
Rowse, G. L., and Wing, P. "Assessing Competitive Structures in Higher Education." *Journal of Higher Education*, 1982, *53* (6), 656–686.
Thompson, J. D. *Organizations in Action*. New York: McGraw-Hill, 1967.
Whetton, D. A. "Interorganizational Relations: A Review of the Field." *Journal of Higher Education*, 1981, *52* (1), 1–27.

Daniel T. Seymour is visiting scholar in the Higher Education Research Institute, University of California, Los Angeles.

The more the boundaries of higher education are blurring, the more they need effective and strategic management.

Openness and Opportunity

Ernest A. Lynton

The basic theme of this sourcebook, well expressed by Seymour in Chapter One, is that the boundaries of academic institutions are changing in ways that challenge campus leaders to manage the boundaries in an active and strategic manner. Just to administer, in a passive fashion, the activities that occur at the boundaries is no longer sufficient.

In his chapter, Seymour discusses a conceptual framework for the management of boundaries. The present chapter explores in greater detail the basic reasons why colleges and universities in recent years have become social institutions that are part of the encompassing structure of the community. It will describe the principal societal trends that are transforming the nature of higher education's boundaries, making them increasingly permeable and the institutions increasingly open, and thereby creating substantial opportunities for exciting and valuable activities but at the same time posing growing challenges for the effective management of institutional boundaries.

The issue is not a new one. A substantial degree of openness has characterized modern American universities from their very inception, during the nineteenth century. Education in this country was linked to societal needs even then. In his 1848 annual report as secretary to the Massachusetts State Board of Education, Horace Mann described schools as "the grand agent for the development or augmentation of national resources, more powerful in the production and gainful employment of the total wealth of a country than all the other things mentioned in the books of the political economists" (Mann, 1848, p. 42). Fourteen years later, in the first major exercise of federal involvement in higher education, the Morrill Act granted land to the states in order to establish colleges that would "promote the liberal and practical education of the industrial classes in the several pursuits and professions of life."

Subsequent federal action soon added a focus on research and on bringing resulting new ideas and techniques to their potential users. In 1887, the federal Hatch Act established agricultural experiment stations, which applied basic science to the solution of specific agricultural problems. Federal support for the Cooperative Extension Service was provided by the Smith-Lever Act in 1914.

Toward the end of the nineteenth century, the growth of graduate education and the increasing role of research indicated a shift of emphasis in American universities, toward knowledge for its own sake and away from a more utilitarian view (see, for example, Veysey, 1965, pp. 173–179). But the institutional boundaries remained permeable. Lord Ashby, widely known British educator, stated in 1967 that "the great American contribution to higher education has been to dismantle the walls around the campus. When President Van Hise of Wisconsin said that the borders of the campus are the boundaries of the state, he put into words one of the rare innovations in the evolution of universities" (Ashby, 1967, p. 4).

Hence, the present interest in managing the boundaries continues a tradition that dates from the nineteenth century. Although the issue is long-standing, conditions today are vastly different in kind and in degree. Both scale and urgency have changed drastically. The sections that follow will explore the principal reasons: on the one hand, the growth of higher education and its consequences in terms of visibility and cost; on the other hand, the emergence of the postindustrial society, with its emphasis on knowledge and its unprecedented need for a well-educated labor force and a steady flow of innovation.

The Consequences of Growth

Just before World War II, in 1939–40, 1,708 colleges and universities enrolled a total of 1.5 million students. In the fall of 1985, 2,009 four-year colleges and universities served 7.7 million students, with an additional 1,292 two-year colleges enrolling another 4.3 million. That represents a doubling of the number of institutions and an increase in students by a factor of eight. Perhaps even more significant than the absolute growth in numbers is the increase in participation rate: in 1980, more than half of all high school graduates continued into full- or part-time higher education. In subsequent years, this rate decreased somewhat, but it remains substantially higher than the 1940 figure of fewer than one in ten.

These changes in the scale of higher education have a number of fundamental consequences with regard to its relationship with external constituencies. In the first place, what happens in colleges and universities has become of interest to a vastly greater number of young people, as well as to their parents and families. The cost of higher education, life on campus, the content of curricula, the availability of jobs for graduates: all this has come to matter to a substantial segment of the population.

That alone would be enough to trigger greater attention by legislators and other governmental officials. In addition, there is the increased demand by public higher education on the public purse. From claiming an almost negligible portion of annual state budgets, the state-funded operating costs of public colleges and universities, together with state funds for student aid, have grown in most states to represent about 5 to 6 percent of public expenditures. That makes the financial needs of higher education very visible; and when resources are limited, higher education is placed in direct competition for scarce funds with other important state activities.

During the years of higher education's expansion, it was both difficult and probably unnecessary to disentangle cause and effect in the relationship between growing college attendance and the concomitant rise in the number of jobs for which a college degree was expected. Regardless of what is the chicken and what is the egg, the fact that employers began to look for college-educated individuals to fill a growing number of jobs added yet another major constituency to the list of those directly affected by higher education.

For all these reasons associated with growth, access to higher education has become an issue of broad concern and thus a trigger for various boundary-spanning activities. The higher the participation rate in higher education, the more nonparticipation becomes debilitating and stigmatizing. Hence, there developed growing pressure for equity in access. This has led to a variety of outreach programs, as well as to collaboration with secondary schools (for example, Project Advance of Syracuse University, mentioned in Chapter One). It has also triggered growing interest among minority advocates and civil rights groups in what higher education is doing to diversify the student body.

No wonder, then, that there has been a sharp increase in external scrutiny across the boundaries of higher education, both at the systemic level and at the level of the individual institution. Parents and students are asking whether a college education is worth the financial sacrifice. Government, representing the public at large, wants to know whether appropriated monies are being wisely spent. Employers voice their expectations that graduates be suitably prepared. Advocates of affirmative action are pressing for better results. From all sides, the pressure for assessment and accountability has increased because of postwar growth in higher education.

This places great demands on the managers of academic boundaries, particularly in terms of two of the six activities discussed by Seymour in Chapter One: *representing* the institution to its external constituencies, and *protecting* it from undue external demands. Inevitably, these demands will exceed the capacity of the institution to deliver, whether with regard to cost containment, affirmative action, or appropriateness of curricula. In most cases, excessive external expectations are based on a limited understanding of the nature of an academic institution. Managers of academic boundaries have the difficult task of explaining institutional constraints to the outside while at the same time convincing an often reluctant internal constituency of the need for change. As in so many other cases of boundary management, success with the internal audience will depend largely on how effective the managers are seen to be with the external audience, and vice versa. Faculties are more willing to modify their procedures and policies if they see their administrators as protecting them against excessive demands, and those exerting pressure from the outside can be more easily persuaded to keep such pressure within bounds if they witness positive administrative leadership within the institution. Moreover, with regard to these boundary-spanning issues (as with most issues to be mentioned in succeeding sections), boundary management must be strategic: it must be based on a clear understanding of institutional responsibilities and mission, and it must strike the appropriate balance for each particular institution.

The Postindustrial Society

The large size and high participation rate that came about during the years between World War II and the early 1970s thus resulted in relating colleges and universities more closely to a variety of external constituencies. Growth made it more important to communicate across the boundaries, but it did not, in and of itself, change the nature of the boundaries. Such a change has come about in recent years, however, as a consequence of the fundamental societal developments that mark the transition into what is variously called the postindustrial, knowledge, or information society. Whatever the label, and however much one discounts the hype spread by some of the gurus of contemporary life, it is evident that the societal importance of both information and knowledge has substantially increased in recent years. This inevitably affects higher education directly because knowledge is the primary concern of our colleges and universities. They are the principal instruments to which society looks for the creation, aggregation, synthesis, interpretation, and dissemination of advanced knowledge. When such knowledge assumes a new importance for both the economic and the political well-being of a country, this inevitably affects the relationship of higher education to the surrounding world. Not only is there the need to increase communication and traffic across the boundaries, but the very nature of these demarcations also changes. As we shall see, higher education can be less and less defined in traditional terms used to describe its timing in the life of an individual, its continuity, or the time, place, or method of its delivery. Furthermore, new conditions raise serious questions about how sacrosanct the autonomy of higher education is and about whether it should have sole authority over the content of what it teaches.

One characteristic of the postindustrial society that primarily affects the nature of higher education's boundaries and its relationships with its external constituencies is the new emphasis on skilled manpower. Mann's (1848) statement, quoted at the beginning of this chapter, indicates that the importance of education to economic vitality was recognized more than a century ago. The industrialization of this country, the growing mechanization of agriculture, and the evolution of complex commercial enterprises increased the need for technical and other professionals. This need has escalated in contemporary society. Exaggerations and simplifications abound in many current statements regarding the relationship of our competitive edge in the global economy to the skills of the labor force, but they contain a substantial core of validity. The shift in employment from the production to the service sector, the move from mass production to flexible specialization, and the pervasive impact of automation have placed an unprecedented premium on education. Hardly a day passes without a pronouncement from a governmental or corporate official, or an article in a national magazine or widely read newspaper calling for the improvement of education at all levels, to enhance the country's competitiveness.

These concerns have already led to a variety of boundary-spanning activities. There has been an increase in general corporate support for higher education, and there have been significant industrial donations of equipment and money in such special areas as computer science, biochemistry, and manufacturing engineering. A recent survey (Conference Board, 1988) indicates that 100 percent of all large manufacturing corporations and 90 percent of all large enterprises have provided material help to higher education. In many cases, such support has created long-term relationships between donors and recipients, which in some few cases have led to effective collaboration in curriculum development and exchanges of staff.

In addition, the growing interest of employers in college-educated individuals has also created new alliances between higher education and business, to raise public awareness about the need for adequate state and federal support for higher education. The Business-Higher Education Forum, for example, started by the American Council on Education, brings together presidents of colleges and universities and chief executive officers of some of the country's leading corporations for joint discussions of shared concerns. Nationally, the forum's periodic reports on the role and needs of higher education have gained substantial visibility and attention; many similar efforts exist at the state and local levels.

Much current concern about higher education focuses on the inadequacy of the basic skills of many college graduates, who cannot express themselves clearly and cannot think critically. In addition, however, one can sense growing recognition of the need to change our basic conception and definition of *competence*. In the postwar decades, industrialized countries were caught up in a veritable cult of the expert. Competence came to be viewed as "knowing more and more about less and less": growing expertise in increasingly specialized and narrowly defined fields. Specialized expertise continues to be important. Indeed, most occupations demand ever greater technological and methodological sophistication. In recent years, however, the limitations of specialization by itself have become more and more apparent. Competence requires more than expertise in a single, well-defined field. The widespread trend toward decentralized organizations and the blurring of hierarchical distinctions are forcing a growing proportion of lower- and middle-level employees to participate actively in decision making. In turn, the growing complexity of issues and the interdependence of technical and social factors have increased the skills needed for these new responsibilities. Individuals need an understanding of the reciprocal interactions between their work and its local, regional, and even international frameworks. Competence depends as much on a broad range of understanding as on expertise in a well-defined technical field. It is significant that the most recent round of review of the undergraduate engineering curriculum at MIT calls for a substantial increase in nontechnical subjects, to make engineers into decision makers, rather than only technical advisers to those in power.

Because of these same trends in working conditions, individuals will increasingly have to work as part of diverse teams and in flexible, frequently shifting organizational patterns. The management of technology also requires close cooperation between technical and nontechnical personnel. These two groups must be able to communicate with each other; they must possess (as it were) reciprocal literacy. Again, these developments broaden the dimensions of competence. They challenge higher education to develop broader programs of preparation, in which breadth and depth will be truly integrated.

The mounting external criticism of excessive specialization in many preprofessional programs is too often expressed in terms that amount to little more than a replay of the perennial and dysfunctional debate between advocates of a broad liberal education and those who stress the necessity of acquiring specialized expertise. On one side, there are those who wish to cram ever more technical subjects into the curriculum; the most extreme among those in opposition tend to say, "Just teach them to think clearly and to express themselves well—everything else, they can learn on the job."

That will simply not do, nor is it sufficient merely to add a number of random, unconnected, general education courses to a narrowly specialized major. Employers as well as educators need to work closely together to reach a shared understanding that depth and breadth must become complementary and reinforcing components of an integrated curriculum. To accomplish this, they will have to overcome two major barriers (a task that will severely test the leadership and boundary-management capabilities of academic administrators). At the boundary with employers, as well as with professional societies and accrediting bodies, academic leaders have the responsibility to press for a broad conception of competence in both preparatory and continuing professional education. There also exist boundaries that must be spanned within the institution. Discipline-bound faculty members must be persuaded to work with their colleagues in other fields to develop integrated programs in which liberal and professional subjects are interrelated and reinforce each other.

A further necessary change in the nature of competence is triggered by the fact that most graduates of our higher education institutions will be called on to make decisions with regard to "messy" and incompletely defined situations. The real problems that they will confront probably will have no single "correct" solutions. In most cases, decision makers will need to choose among several approaches, each of which will have both advantages and drawbacks. Our current didactic approach in higher education does not prepare graduates to deal with reality in this fashion. They do not know how to deal with trade-offs among competing outcomes. We educate future practitioners as if they were going to apply exact sciences. The deductive approach of most college teaching suggests that all real-life situations can be reduced to well-defined problems, which can be analyzed and solved exactly through the use of broadly applicable principles. Unfortunately, reality is more complex, and the practice of most professions and occupations is not an exact science. If higher education is to do a better job of preparing individuals for effective and competent practice, it needs to become more inductive in its teaching and to make better use of practical experience as a primary source of learning. Again, this suggests new modes of cooperation between higher education and various external constituencies, as well as a blurring of the traditional boundaries.

New Patterns of Education

The Transition from Education to Work. The importance of employing highly skilled individuals, together with acute shortages of graduates in certain areas of engineering and management, has also triggered, almost inadvertently, new patterns of transition from education to work. These in turn create both the need and the opportunity for new linkages between higher education and employers. Because of the shortage of qualified entrants into the labor force, there is sufficient demand to cause many young people with baccalaureate degrees lucrative job offers in these fields. The opportunity cost of continuing full-time study is too great. With the baccalaureate, they can carry out entry-level tasks in their occupations while they pursue master's degrees on a part-time basis. This does not constitute continuing education in the traditional sense; the master's degree continues to be the real professional preparation. Instead of pursuing it in a continuous, full-time mode, however, students in management and engineering increasingly enter a spread-out pattern of advanced education, which combines work and learning.

A similar development may well occur during the coming years with regard to the last two years of undergraduate study. Demographic factors are rapidly reducing the number of young people entering the job market for jobs that traditionally were filled by college graduates. As a result, we may soon see that individuals who have finished only the first two years of college will receive job offers that they cannot afford to turn down. This will create a substantial demand for opportunities to complete the latter years of an undergraduate program on a part-time basis. Close collaboration between employers and educators will again be of great importance.

Additional pressures may speed the move toward new patterns of education in the transition from school to work. The need for a more inclusive conception of professional competence and the resulting need for broader educational programs are coming at a time when more and more material of a specialized nature must also be included, to provide appropriate expertise. There is no way of fitting all of this into the educational process unless one either lengthens it substantially or develops new patterns. The former is no solution. In most countries, there already exist complaints about the length of the programs of study in many professional and occupational areas; hence, it is necessary to reconsider the basic approach of higher education and to stop trying to cram all necessary knowledge and skills into the preemployment, preparatory phase. Increasingly, we should conceptualize the introductory process of career development as combining a first, preemployment stage with a structured, part-time supplement to be pursued during the first years on the job.

It is obvious that such a trend toward new patterns of transition from education to work calls for closer linkages between employers and educators. At the minimum, some degree of communication is needed so as to schedule time and place of instruction for the optimal convenience of all concerned. In many cases, there is much closer collaboration: often classes are actually scheduled on the premises of an employer; in recent years, there has also been rapid expansion of televised instruction. Many colleges and universities have their own systems of producing and disseminating videotapes or of beaming instruction directly to corporate sites by microwave transmission. A national consortium of engineering schools, working closely with a number of leading high-technology industries, has created the National Technological University, which makes available entire master's degree-level curricula in various areas of engineering by means of satellite transmission.

All of these efforts require various modes of boundary management. In addition to many housekeeping and logistical matters that must be arranged collaboratively, there are quite a few issues in which the interests of employers and educational institutions may diverge. Contention can arise with regard to admissions and registration, as well as with regard to evaluations and final grades. There can be conflicts of time between the requirements of the job and the demands of the instructional program. Some issues can be settled easily; others will test the adaptive skills of managers on both sides, particularly the skills of academic administrators.

Lifelong Maintenance of Competence. A distributed pattern for the initial portions of occupational and professional development sets the stage for an even more fundamental need: a recurrent pattern of formal instruction throughout an individual's active life is made necessary by the acceleration of change and the rapid obsolescence of knowledge and understanding. Investments in human resources must be protected by ongoing intellectual maintenance. The need for this goes beyond coping with the introduction of new techniques and other innovations. Change occurs in many different ways. Given the growing interdependence of technical, social, economic, and political factors, as well as the increasing internationalization of commerce, an effective practitioner needs to keep up to date in all of the pertinent fields. Furthermore, change occurs not just at the level of facts, figures, and methods; basic concepts and theories become outdated, and new ones need to be learned. To expect individuals to accomplish this on their own is neither realistic nor cost-effective. It can best be done in the way in which fundamental understanding was first imparted: through organized instruction.

The challenges created by these new needs are particularly great for the higher education community. It needs to respond to the continually evolving developmental demand with an unprecedented degree of speed and flexibility. In addition, it must create modular approaches to curriculum that can provide some degree of coherence and accumulation of learning to a series of short courses and workshops. The need for close and continuing cooperation between employers and educators is particularly important in the development and delivery of such lifelong and recurrent education. Of necessity, the pattern of such intellectual maintenance must be closely integrated into the work of the participating individuals, in terms of content and with regard to time, place, and format of instruction.

In view of the fact that financial support can constitute one form of linkage across the boundaries, it is worth noting that employers each year spend $30 billion or more on education and training of their employees, an amount that exceeds the total expenditures of all fifty states for instructional costs in public higher education (see, for example, Lynton, 1984). Corporate emphasis on employee development is steadily increasing (Lusterman, 1985) and continues to offer substantial opportunities for colleges and universities. Chapter Three will further discuss boundary-spanning activities involving employee education.

About $2 billion annually of corporate expenditures go toward tuition for regular courses taken by employees. This amount already constitutes a major source of tuition revenue for higher education, yet employee participation in tuition reimbursement plans is still low. Experience in a number of corporations (see, for example, Barton, 1982) has shown that many more employees would take advantage of such benefits if they were provided with appropriate information and guidance. As yet, far too few colleges and universities have provided such services.

An Alternative Path from Secondary to Higher Education. For different reasons, the time may also be ripe to develop in this country alternative patterns of education for young people who have finished tenth grade. The nature of what used to be blue- and white-collar jobs has changed as a result of the impact of technology on the workplace. In the past, many shop-floor and office jobs required little more than manual skills, and they could be filled by individuals with secondary vocational education. Increasingly, however, as jobs change from the direct manipulation of tools and machines to the electronic control of such devices, knowing why is becoming as important as knowing how. Increasingly, too, the automated workplace, both in the service and manufacturing sectors, requires smart workers as well as "smart" machines. Thus, there is a growing need for "blue-and-white-striped collar" workers, low-level technicians who combine substantial manipulative skills with a considerable amount of conceptual understanding at the postsecondary level.

Another factor pertinent to this level of education is that many young people—not only those in inner-city schools—become tired of being in school full-time by the time they reach tenth grade. Under present conditions, the educational system of this country offers essentially no alternatives beyond either staying in high school or dropping out. An alternative pathway should exist, which would not carry the lasting stigma of dropping out and would provide a structured opportunity to continue education while holding a job.

Experience in a number of European countries has indicated the value of an employment-based system that combines formal schooling, technical instruction, and on-the-job training, starting from approximately the tenth-grade level and progressing to the equivalent of the first or second year of community college. Interest in programs that straddle the secondary and postsecondary levels has been growing in this country as well. A 2 + 2 program, combining the last two years of secondary education with two years of community college, as long advocated by Parnell (1985), has been introduced at La Guardia Community Colleges and is being replicated in a number of other institutions. Federal legislation for the support of such "tech-prep" education will be introduced as part of the impending reconsideration of the Perkins Vocational Education Act.

The existing experimental programs in this country already have a strong work component but are still primarily school based. Employment-based work-and-education programs, such as exist in some European countries, are an even more exciting possibility. Clearly, it will require an unprecedented degree of active collaboration among employers, unions, government officials, and educators, with many potential bones of contention at the boundaries.

A Common Need: Strategic Management of the Boundaries. What the existing as well as the anticipated developments described in the preceding sections have in common is that they all constitute a basic change in the traditional pattern of education. To date, it is customary for learning to precede doing and for formal education to be completed before the start of a career. But this is changing, and the trend is clearly toward ever greater overlap between learning and working. Indeed, a number of writers envision a future in which the two are completely intertwined. For example, a proposal by a special committee of MIT's Department of Electrical Engineering and Computer Science (Bruce and others, 1982) calls for "lifelong cooperative education," which entails an almost symbiotic relationship between practicing engineers and their academic colleagues in what the authors call "an extended academic community." The result would include:

- Replacement of the present discontinuity between full-time study and full-time work by a gradual transition extending through most of the professional life of an engineer
- Joint sharing by industry and engineering schools of the responsibility for the continuing education or working engineers
- Intermixing of work, teaching, and study with the active support of employers [Bruce and others, 1982, p. 32].

The vision of the MIT group may strike many as utopian, a goal toward which one can strive, but which will never be fully reached.

Others may view it, with alarm, as the ultimate disappearance of academic autonomy. Yet the fact that it constitutes a serious proposal from a serious source indicates that there exist many good reasons (as well as substantial pressures) to bring about a substantial reduction of the traditional demarcation in time between education and work, with an increasing amount of overlap and coordination between the two. Further pressures, as well as good reasons, are added by the need (mentioned earlier, in the discussion of competence) to introduce more practical experiences at an early stage into even the traditional educational patterns.

The preceding sections combine to suggest that colleges and universities are currently at the threshold of what could be very fundamental changes in their instructional activities, in ways that profoundly affect the nature of education, as well as relationships to and interactions with external constituencies. Working together with these constituencies, institutions that dare to cross that threshold may achieve a synergism of education and work, in which the combination of the two adds more to the development of an individual than does the sum of each separately. There are risks in moving too far and too fast and, above all, in allowing growth of boundary-spanning activities without careful consideration of their long-term strategic implications and without provisions for active management. There are also substantial risks in standing pat and ignoring changing societal conditions and needs. Striking the right balance, moving at a pace and in a direction consistent with institutional capabilities and goals: these have always been the challenges of proper boundary management with regard to the instructional mission of colleges and universities. In this postindustrial society, they have acquired an unprecedented urgency and scope. In the sections that follow, we shall see that the same situation exists in scholarly and professional activities.

The Ongoing Quest for Innovation

Collaboration in Research and Development. An additional dramatic increase in the permeability of the boundaries of higher education has come about in the area of research and development. Two characteristics of this postindustrial era have caused this to happen: the pervasive need for a steady flow of innovative products and services to maintain economic competitiveness, and the shrinking time between basic research and its practical applications. To beat the competition to new ideas and new techniques, business and industry must establish close relationships with universities, which continue to be a principal focus of basic and applied research. As a result, collaboration in this area has escalated in less than a decade, from existing at an almost negligible level to becoming a major factor in financing university research and influencing its directions.

There exists a wide variety of boundary-spanning activities in research. On a scale of intensity of collaboration, corporate financial support for research, with few or no strings attached, is at the low end. This kind of collaboration has increased substantially in recent years, although it continues to be less pervasive than research funding from federal sources. In some cases, large corporations have made major multi-year commitments to leading universities so as to encourage the development or strengthening of specific research directions, with the understanding that corporate scientists would have free access to the research and that donor corporations would have free licenses to any resulting patents. The relationships of Monsanto to Harvard and of Exxon to MIT (see Chapter One) are two examples. A large number of engineering schools, as well as some science departments, invite corporations to become associates: in return for a yearly donation, a company's representatives receive periodic briefings on research in progress. In addition, participating employers usually have early and easy access to graduate students as possible employees and to faculty as possible consultants.

A further degree of cooperation exists in the growing number of cooperative research centers. Many of these were started under a National Science Foundation program; more recently, a number of states have provided appropriate incentives, and some of these centers have been started by the collaborating partners without outside subvention. The units (such as Stanford University's Center for Integrated Systems, cited in Chapter One) are university laboratories in specific fields, jointly financed by a group of industrial sponsors, with ongoing and frequent contact between academic and corporate colleagues. In a number of research institutes and centers administered by academic-industrial consortia, research and development are carried out by teams of corporate and university scientists and engineers. Dimancescu and Botkin (1986) describe fourteen of these "new alliances." They vary considerably in organization and management, but they all represent a boundary-spanning relationship that is both close and complex, so that at times it is difficult to define the line of demarcation, and this places substantial demands on managerial skills.

Commercialization. Boundaries also become obscured, and management complicated, through a second consequence of the continuing demand for innovation and the shrinking time between research and its applications. This consequence is the strong pressure on academic researchers (and on their institutions) to commercialize new techniques and new products coming out of university laboratories. Most research universities have established or enlarged one kind of important boundary-spanning mechanism: special offices, staffed by technical as well as legal experts, that undertake the often arduous process of obtaining patents for research results. Often, these offices are also involved in marketing licenses to university patents.

The rush to commercialize has also led to a proliferation of spinoff ventures, in which university researchers often have financial interest. To facilitate the development of such enterprises, a number of universities have established "incubation centers" on or near their campuses—sites where the fledgling ventures can rent space, use common technical and other support services, and have ready access to faculty and graduate students, as well as to library and computer facilities. Some well-endowed universities even participate directly as investors in the capitalization of new ventures.

These activities can contribute to universities both intellectually and financially, and they also have great potential value to the economy as a whole, but they constitute a boundary terrain so new and so unexplored that no one is quite sure where to position the demarcations. Internally, how does one distinguish between the priorities of an academic institution and the interests of a commercial investor, as well as between faculty members as scholars and as entrepreneurs? Externally, where does one draw the line between the university and its commercial partners? These developments have forced universities to examine closely issues of intellectual property, patent rights, and potential conflicts of interest. Considerable experience has been acquired by university and corporate officials in recent years in dealing with such matters (see, for example, Betz, 1988; Dimancescu and Botkin, 1986; Fairweather, 1988), but these issues constitute a continuing challenge to the managers of boundaries.

Technology Transfer. The creation of scientific and technical innovation through research and development, and the commercialization of the results through new high-tech ventures, are only part of a complex and challenging process that is needed to enhance a country's competitiveness. In this information- and technology-intensive era, it is equally important to maintain the vitality of existing enterprises by means of ongoing modernization through absorption of new equipment and techniques. We cannot afford to abandon our matured manufacturing base, which has already been seriously eroded by our neglect in recent years. We must also keep existing service deliverers at the cutting edge of innovation. To accomplish this, we need to aggregate and synthesize the outcomes of basic and applied research and then to disseminate and apply them throughout the public and private sectors of the economy. At the same time, and largely through the same channels of communication, issues and problems arising in practice need to be fed back, often to the most basic level of research.

In short, we need to pay more attention to *technology transfer,* a term that was first used to describe the flow of innovation from industrialized to less developed countries. The same concept now applies to the mature sectors of the economy of an industrialization country. The accelerating pace of technical and scientific innovation can leave existing businesses and industries—and public-sector agencies as well—underdeveloped, in a very real sense, unless they benefit from a steady and effective transfer of new knowledge. Maintaining the competitiveness of our older industries is as important as creating ventures in new fields. In the global competition with other industrialized countries, we lag behind not only in many high-tech fields but also in such sectors as machine tools and textile machinery—all but dead here, and thriving elsewhere.

In our current discussions about competitiveness, we tend to overlook one part of the economy in which this country has been and continues to be spectacularly competitive: agriculture. Indeed, American agriculture is at this time the victim of its own success. That our agriculture has always remained at the cutting edge of technology and has steadily improved its productivity is largely due to a remarkable American invention in higher education: combining agricultural experiment stations and agricultural extension, and thus creating a close connection between sources of new knowledge and effective mechanisms for its dissemination. In agriculture, we have recognized that ongoing technology transfer is a complex, multifaceted, two-way process connecting the creation of new knowledge with its ultimate utilization. Until recently, most faculty members in schools of agriculture were engaged in outreach as well as research and instruction, an arrangement reflecting the close interrelationships among these three components of technology transfer. This multiple and interconnected function of schools of agriculture has been sustained by federal funds since the 1887 Hatch Act and the 1914 Smith-Lever Act.

The post-Sputnik emphasis on basic research, as well as the resulting availability of generous federal funds, reduced the interest of our universities in extension activities. Although we continue to pay lip service to the triad of research, service, and teaching, the tradition established in agriculture has not been extended to other areas. On the contrary, the prestige and the rewards in the academic world are all concentrated on basic research. Paradoxically, West Germany and certain other industrialized nations have remembered in recent years what we have forgotten: the need for explicit policies and procedures to enhance the transfer of new ideas and techniques from the research laboratory to where they can be used. As one U.S. corporate executive remarked recently after a visit to Baden-Württemberg, one of the states of West Germany, "The U.S. tends to define innovation as invention; Germany defines innovation as the application of invention." The federal and the state governments in West Germany provide support for a variety of activities and organizations, which together constitute an effective industrial extension service.

It is high time that higher education in the United States also applied the lessons of its own past and gave as great an emphasis (and as high a status) to the dissemination and application of new knowledge as to its creation. There are some encouraging signs of growing interest and activity with regard to a modern version of extension.

Public initiatives exist in just about every state of this country. For example, the Benjamin Franklin Partnership Program in Pennsylvania provides matching funds to help support a number of advanced technology centers at academic institutions, which conduct applied research in close collaboration with industry. In addition, Pennsylvania State University has a substantial technology extension service called PENNTAP. Similarly, in Ohio, the Thomas Edison Program supports technology centers as well as an extension service called OTTO. Many additional examples of applied research centers and of local or regional technology extension networks can be found in other states.

The examples of successful technology extension in this country indicate the crucial importance of an effective infrastructure that serves as a boundary-spanning mechanism and catalyst for the relationship between academic institutions and the potential users of their technical expertise. Two aspects are particularly important.

The first is to make our universities and colleges more transparent to outsiders. At this time, it is usually very difficult to find out the areas of faculty interest and the kinds of technical assistance that may be available. In several European countries, every university has a "contact office" that provides this service, and a number of universities in this country have also successfully instituted such a mechanism.

The second important aspect involves the need for effective extension to take the initiative in reaching out, particularly to the smaller private enterprises and public agencies. In the area of technology transfer, these constitute the equivalent of the nontraditional student in the area of instruction. For both, special measures must be taken to encourage access. In agricultural extension, active outreach by extension agents enhances access for small farmers and other constituencies at the lower end of the agricultural economy. The equivalent is needed in industrial extension.

Many choices need to be made in organizing these various types of boundary-spanning mechanisms: whether to do it centrally or in a decentralized fashion, whether to use faculty only or also to rely on special technical staff, whether and how to compensate faculty, whether and how to use students (Lynton and Elman, 1987; Crosson, 1989.) The resolution of such issues can have an appreciable effect on the institution; these are not minor procedural or organizational details. For public institutions, there exist further delicate questions regarding the extent to which services will be provided pro bono; and all colleges and universities share the inevitable dilemma that to make the institution available as a source of technical information and advice is inevitably to raise excessive expectations. Thus, again, active and strategic management of boundaries is required.

Conclusion

A basic theme runs through this chapter: the impact of contemporary societal changes may affect not just the periphery of academic institutions but also their central core. The pressures arising from the central importance of knowledge; the shortage of skilled manpower; the accelerating rate of technological and other changes; the resulting need for the lifelong renewal of competence, as well as for technology transfer; incentives to commercialize research findings—each of these can bring about fundamental changes in either the instructional or the scholarly role (or both) of colleges and universities. Many of them have already been substantially affected; few if any will remain unchanged. In many ways and for many reasons, the prospects and opportunities are exciting. They provide the possibilities of invigorating new tasks and new relationships.

But there also exist considerable dangers. One can move too fast or too slowly, too far or not far enough. For each academic institution, there is an optimal extent and pace of change, which depends on its current circumstances, its resources, and its long-term goals. The greatest danger of all would be to look at the trees and ignore the forest, to administer a variety of boundary-spanning activities and ignore the important long-range issues that are involved and the strategic choices that must be made. Indeed, the changing boundaries of our academic institutions must be actively and aggressively managed.

References

Ashby, E. "The Case for Ivory Towers." Paper presented to the International Conference on Higher Education in Tomorrow's World, Ann Arbor, Mich., Apr. 26-29, 1967.

Barton, P. *Worklife Transition: The Adult Learning Connection.* New York: McGraw-Hill, 1982.

Betz, F. "Partnerships for Research: Lessons from Experience." In D. R. Powers, M. F. Powers, F. Betz, and C. B. Aslanian (eds.), *Higher Education in Partnership with Industry: Opportunities and Strategies for Training, Research, and Economic Development.* San Francisco: Jossey-Bass, 1988.

Bruce, J. D., Siebert, W. M., Smullin, L. D., and Fano, R. M. *Lifelong Cooperative Education.* Cambridge, Mass.: MIT Press, 1982.

Conference Board. "Corporate-University Relations Programs." *Perspectives*, 1988, *14*, entire issue.

Crosson, P. "Rendering Professional Service." Unpublished paper, National Association of State Universities and Land Grant Colleges, 1989.

Dimancescu, D., and Botkin, J. *The New Alliance: America's R & D Consortia.* Cambridge, Mass.: Ballinger, 1986.

Fairweather, J. S. *Entrepreneurship and Higher Education: Lessons for Colleges, Universities, and Industry.* ASHE-ERIC Higher Education Research Report no. 6. Washington, D.C.: Association for the Study of Higher Education, 1988.

Lusterman, S. *Trends in Corporate Education and Training.* Report no. 870. New York: Conference Board, 1985.

Lynton, E. *The Missing Connection Between Business and the Universities.* New York: ACE/Macmillan, 1984.

Lynton, E. A., and Elman, S. E. *New Priorities for the University: Meeting Society's Needs for Applied Knowledge and Competent Individuals.* San Francisco: Jossey-Bass, 1987.

Mann, H. *Eleventh Annual Report of the Board of Education, Together with the Eleventh Annual Report of the Secretary.* Boston: Dutton and Wentworth, 1848.

Parnell, D. *The Neglected Majority.* Washington, D.C.: Community College Press, 1985.

Veysey, L. *The Emergence of the American University.* Chicago: University of Chicago Press, 1965.

Ernest A. Lynton is Commonwealth Professor at the University of Massachusetts, Boston, and senior associate of its New England Resource Center for Higher Education in the John W. McCormack Institute of Public Affairs.

Institutions of higher education are being profoundly influenced by collaborations with business and industry, but rarely oversee these relationships using a strategic boundary management approach.

Managing the New Frontier Between Colleges and Companies

Lee Teitel

Colleges and universities are now involved in types of collaborations with businesses and industries that were almost unheard of fifteen or even ten years ago. As Lynton has noted in Chapter Two, this is a change both of scale and of degree. While it is becoming increasingly commonplace for community colleges to offer customized job training for companies, pathbreaking institutions are offering a dazzling array of services, including operating as personnel agents for companies—recruiting, screening, and training their new employees. Similarly, while more and more university departments provide focused research for corporate sponsors, a few are forming significant, precedent-setting, joint partnerships with, for instance, biotechnology companies to develop commercial applications arising from faculty members' research.

The increased depth and breadth of these relationships unleash powerful forces that have the potential for a significant impact on the evolution of the educational institutions and create new demands on their boundary-management capabilities.

In this chapter, I advance the following three propositions:

1. The boundary between the academic and the corporate worlds is in an unprecedented state of flux. The line between what colleges will and will not do for business and industry is constantly shifting. These changes go on within an institution when one department approves of a professor's external connections while another refuses to provide the same latitude to its faculty members (Fox, 1981). Furthermore, because the academy is far from monolithic, sometimes what one university will not agree to do, another will. Lepkowski (1981, p. 31) describes an example: "Washington University is doing something which Harvard rejected and Stanford has said it will not do. It is using university funds to establish business enterprises."

2. The increased involvement with business and industry has an enormous potential impact on institutions of higher education. At a community college, this can mean the concentrated influence on the approach to curriculum, training, education, and staffing that the growing and profitable business- and industry-oriented programs have. At a research university, it can mean the impact that corporate financing and needs for secrecy have on the research direction, dissemination of information, and departmental structure of the institution.

3. Although structures have been put into place to *facilitate* the transactions that go on at this critical boundary point for academia, colleges may not be successfully addressing the need to *manage* the boundary with the long-term interests of the institutions in mind.

In this chapter, I will briefly describe this change in relationship and suggest some of its implications for boundary management. The first section highlights some of the factors detailed in Chapter Two that have contributed to the trend toward seeking opportunities through collaboration. The second section provides a sampling of leading-edge partnership examples. The third section examines the structures put in place by educational institutions to facilitate and encourage these interactions. The fourth section explores the existing and potential impact of these business- and industry-oriented activities on institutions of higher education that engage in them. The chapter concludes with a look at the boundary-management tasks that are necessary for colleges and universities and with the suggestion that these tasks are not being—and cannot be—properly addressed by the organizational structures that exist.

Roots of the New Partnerships

For much of this century, potentially symbiotic involvements of colleges and corporations have been conducted at arm's length or else have been held in check by a fairly well defined boundary between the organizations. With the growth of federal support for research in the 1950s supplanting relatively low levels of corporate support, and with the distrust of big business generated on many college campuses during the Vietnam War era, these boundaries became even less permeable (Bok, 1982). With few exceptions (MIT and Stanford come to mind in the research arena, the community colleges of North and South Carolina in the instructional arenas), differing organizational structures, senses of mission, and operating strategies maintained substantial distance between colleges and companies.

The confluence of several major changes in the environment (see Chapter Two) has led to the significant shakeup of this pattern. Economic downturns and the increased sense of competition with Japan have made some companies turn to academia for help in increasing the productivity of their workforces and bringing about more rapid development of new knowledge into marketable applications. Growing awareness of demographic changes in the workforce have increased corporate perception of the need for upgrading and retraining existing workers at the same time that competitive demands on productivity have added a strong sense of urgency to the retraining task. While many of the larger corporations have developed their own elaborate internal training structures (Eurich, 1985), some of them, along with smaller and medium-size companies, have turned to colleges, especially community colleges, to assist in the retraining effort. No longer content with the longer view of exerting a moderate amount of influence by sitting on advisory boards in occupational programs that may eventually produce students for their companies, many officials are taking the more immediate step of contracting with colleges for training of existing employees, an arrangement often referred to as *customized job training*.

Similarly, companies impatient with supporting loosely focused pure research or limited practical research are forming new types of relationships with research universities to pursue focused pure research, applied research, or even technology transfer—getting products developed and to market. Uniquely intimate patterns of sharing royalties from discoveries are being formed as these relationships are being fueled by a sense of the tremendous profits potentially involved.

For their part, colleges are responding to changes in the environment by being much more willing than even ten years ago to seek relationships and opportunities with companies. Concerned about demographic information that foretold a decline in traditional-age students, affected by cutbacks in federal funding, encouraged by state policies that promote collegiate roles in economic development, interested in helping in what has been seen as the country's productivity crisis, and seeing the opportunity for increased revenues for themselves, some colleges and universities have displayed an amazing flexibility and willingness to redefine the frontier between themselves and the corporate world.

Two important caveats must be mentioned about the research reported here. First, when I write about the willingness of colleges and universities to do this or of business and industry to do that, bear in mind that neither of these sectors is monolithic. Decisions about how much and what kind of collaboration to undertake get played out among thousands of dyads, triads, and consortia across the country. Companies may be large or small; institutions of higher education include the whole gamut of community colleges, liberal arts colleges, and research universities. It is important to note that even while great changes are being made on the boundary or frontier between the sectors, many of the colleges and companies in this country are not yet directly involved. A second caveat on generalizations is also in order. Throughout the chapter, most of the examples of instructional relationships between colleges and companies illustrate those established by community colleges; most of the examples of research partnerships are drawn from relatively few well-known research universities. This is not to say that there is no business- and industry-oriented instruction at the university and no research capability at the community college, nor is it to say that nothing at all is going on at the four-year institutions or other universities (for activities at the state colleges, see, for instance, American Association of State Colleges and Universities, 1988). Rather, these examples have been chosen to highlight the two types of institutions that have been at the cutting edge of collaboration in certain areas.

The Depth and Breadth of Change

Contract training and *customized job training* are terms used by community colleges for programs set up specifically to provide instruction for employees of a company. Courses are often noncredit, are frequently delivered on company premises, and are usually shorter and less theoretical than regular community college courses (Kopecek, 1984). Accordingly, the employer usually has a great deal of input into the selection of faculty, the development of the curriculum, and the methods of instructional delivery.

The delivery of these courses is not new; for more than twenty-five years, North and South Carolina have been successfully using the promise of training workers inexpensively as a lure for companies to relocate (*Shadows in the Sunbelt*, 1986). When the Carolinas started their postsecondary technical institutes, as they were called then (most are now called community colleges), they were outside the mainstream of what many considered the junior college movement. An activity that was outside the mainstream has become, in the last ten years, both widespread and embedded as a legitimate part of the mission of the comprehensive community college, and it has become a large segment of what some colleges do. For instance, thirty-six colleges surveyed in 1986 offered a total of almost a thousand courses to over seven hundred companies (Golattscheck, McKenney, and Mahoney, 1986). One indication of the breadth of this movement is the number of community colleges that report having set up offices to coordinate business and industry (B/I) programming, which rose from about 5 percent in 1980 to 50 percent in 1985 and has continued to grow. B/I directors and their staffs promote, coordinate, and often provide the range of business- and industry-oriented activities at the college. Finally, the notion of using collegiate programs for economic development, begun in the Carolinas, is now a matter of state policy in all but six states (National Governors Association, 1986).

In addition to the widespread nature of this "nuts and bolts" type of industry training, a number of institutions go well beyond this model. Each year, the Keep America Working Task Force of the American Association of Community and Junior Colleges gives awards to three community colleges for their work with business and industry. For example, Portland Community College (Oregon) has been recognized for the delivery or administration of all of the education or training programs for Tektronix's twelve thousand employees. This includes customized training, as well as coordination of outside vendors and other educational systems. Greenville Technical College (South Carolina) and Michelin Corporation have built a jointly owned training facility on the Greenville campus. The tire company will use it during the day, the community college at night. Des Moines Area College (Iowa) has been cited for assisting Greyhound Corporation in intake-screening assessment of four thousand applicants for seven hundred jobs at a facility that the company was opening. Over 140 staff members of the college were involved in this screening and in the subsequent training and education programs. Delta Community College (Michigan) developed a program for the training of General Motors dealership personnel that has developed into a nationwide network of more than thirty-five community colleges in twenty-six states (Keep America Working Task Force, 1986, 1987, 1988). These are just four examples of programs that go beyond what has now become the model for such partnerships.

Another college on the cutting edge of this business- and industry-oriented activity is Rio Salado Community College, part of the Maricopa Community College system (Arizona). It is oriented completely toward B/I service, has only five full-time faculty members and no campus, and serves twenty thousand students (Jaschik, 1986).

To place the experiences of these cutting-edge institutions into perspective, recall the role, twenty-five or thirty years ago, of the technical institutes of the Carolinas. What was then as unusual activity, placing them substantially outside the mainstream, is now commonplace and legitimate. The five examples just cited can be seen as the leading edge of a movement that is progressing steadily toward greater collegiate involvement with the corporate sector. The more colleges do with and for companies, the greater the breakdown in organizational boundaries and institutional barriers to further collaboration. An important trade-off is reduction of institutional autonomy, an issue to which I will return.

Research connections between universities and companies can also be viewed as a continuum, with one end constantly moving toward increased involvement with the corporate world. Zinser (1985) provides an excellent summary of the categories that these activities fall into, listed from the most distant connections to the most institutionally intimate (notice how the time-honored affiliation of numbers 1 and 2 coexist with and grow simultaneously with the more leading-edge connections of numbers 5 or 6, as the latter come to the forefront:

1. *Contributions:* These are nonrestrictive gifts by companies to sponsor research activities. Their absolute dollar value has grown steadily for the last four decades, to about 6 percent of university research and development, although the relative percentage of overall research dollars has varied with the influx and the subsequent ebb of federal dollars.

2. *Procurement:* This category involves contracts for specified goods or services—product testing, for instance, or access to university labs for other development purposes.

3. *Linkage:* These arrangements are made through sponsored program offices, which essentially provide information about and coordination between faculty and laboratory resources and company needs.

4. *Exchange:* This category includes trade of assets (tangible or intangible)—for example, technology licensing programs, or industry affiliate programs, whereby the company pays a fee to get a "window" on the university's technological progress.

5. *Cooperative ventures:* These are specific involvements with clearly predefined money and benefits for each party. Many research agreements fall into this category, either through one-to-one relationships (as in the $50 million Massachusetts General Hospital–Hoechst agreement) or through research consortia (some sponsored by the National Science Foundation, others by academic or industrial groups).

6. *Partnerships:* In these arrangements, universities and companies share potential profits and losses. These arrangements usually take one of two major forms. The first involves joint partnerships with established companies (for example, the nonprofit Center for Biotechnology Research of Stanford and the University of California with the for-profit Eugenics, along with six other sponsoring firms). The goals of a joint partnership may be not only to provide long-term research funding, quick technology transfer, and return on investments to the participating companies but also to provide a significant financial return on the companies' commercial activity to the universities. In the second form, the university goes more directly into business. Examples include the University of Roches-

ter's venture capital arm, as well as the University City Science Center, an incubator for faculty projects where clerical, accounting, and contract-negotiation services for faculty entrepreneurs are provided by the University of Pennsylvania. Another direct approach is the wholly (or partly) owned business partnership with the university's own faculty. This model was rejected by Harvard but is in place at Washington University.

As the arm's-length relationships of contribution and procurement are transformed into more embracing cooperative ventures and partnerships, the issues of autonomy, research direction and control, secrecy, and departmental oversight become increasingly important. The next section describes the structures that have been established to facilitate interaction across the boundary between colleges and companies.

Structures

Community colleges and universities have developed very different kinds of structures to facilitate business- and industry-oriented activities. Community colleges with substantial B/I programs tend to channel these activities through business and industry subunits with a high level of autonomy and the ability to exercise significant control over the corporate-academic interface. In contrast, university interactions with companies are more diffuse: individual faculty members can usually cross the border easily, and the wide range of models for activities mitigates against any strong boundary control.

In most community colleges, the principal gatekeepers and managers of the collegiate programs with business and industry are the B/I directors or coordinators. Sometimes their offices are called "Centers for Business and Industry" or "Centers for Economic Development." The B/I directors and their staffs are responsible for promoting the colleges' services to regional companies (or for responding to requests from companies). They are responsible for finding people to meet the instructional or other needs of the companies and for writing up and overseeing the contracts that are involved. (Unless otherwise noted, this discussion of community colleges' practices follows closely findings reported in Teitel, 1988).

Often a B/I office is run through the college's division of continuing education; sometimes it reports to the academic dean, sometimes directly to the president. In an effort to minimize confusion and facilitate systematic contact with the private sector, most campuses with substantial B/I programs designate their B/I units as exclusive liaisons to local companies. Consequently, although a great deal of unofficial consulting on the part of faculty members may go on outside its purview, a B/I unit has a high level of control over the officially designated activities of the college. This had led to tensions at colleges where, before the formation of B/I units, academic departments had offered some of their courses directly to business and industry. The departments frequently have been reluctant to cease their efforts or to funnel them through the B/I units.

In addition to being exclusive contact points, many B/I units function with a great deal of independence and autonomy. Contrary to what one might expect, the B/I unit of XYZ Community College may actually employ none of XYZ's regular faculty members for its courses; in fact, it may deliver all of its courses at the company worksite, using outside consultants to teach and develop the courses. Indeed, many B/I units are virtually autonomous ("We are in our own little world over here," reports one B/I director), running active and highly regarded programs in the business community, but with no contact or even visibility on their own campuses. Relatively few B/I units are integrated into their community colleges. In the few that are, as much as half of the instructional contracts for B/I work go to regular college faculty, and B/I activities are a much better known and discussed part of campus life.

The extensive use of outsiders as supplements to (or replacements for) regular-division faculty members exists for a variety of practical reasons (such as scheduling problems or the unavailability of full-timers on short notice), but it is also motivated by attitudinal factors—for example, the common perception among B/I directors that full-timers are not as up-to-date in their fields or are too theoretical or are not sufficiently skilled to teach adults properly in the work setting. In fact, the boundary spanners themselves—the B/I units—often come to resemble, in culture, attitudes, and organizational structure, the companies with which they work more than the colleges that house them. (For a fuller discussion of how B/I units develop policies and structures—including the extensive use of outsiders—that minimize internal tensions and make spanning the gap to companies easier, see Chapter 4).

This policy of frequently using outsiders has, along with its associated organizational differentiation, three main effects that are significant here. First, it allows the B/I unit's offerings to be more client-centered than resource-based. Lynton and Elman (1987) make an important distinction between these two modes of operation. The resource-based mode draws on the existing strengths of the institutions and attempts to present them to the business and industrial community. The client-based mode, toward which most large-scale community colleges B/I units strive, puts the college in the position of trying to meet any of the instructional (and sometimes other) needs of companies. Second, the use of outsiders gives the B/I unit a high degree of autonomy in establishing what it will or will not do for a corporate client; if B/I units drew exclusively on college faculty, faculty members would have a much greater say in determining where that line is. Furthermore, when it offers much of its programming on a noncredit basis, the B/I unit bypasses the need for any course-approval process. These factors, combined (in many cases) with relative lack of knowledge about what the B/I unit does), give the B/I unit almost unfettered authority over its own negotiations with business and industry. Third, the use of outsiders creates within the college a differentiated subunit, which is typically less collegial and more hierarchical in its organization; it is more responsive to outside influence and more willing to share decision making with outsiders. Furthermore, a B/I unit often runs leaner and more profit-oriented operations than the rest of the college. These characteristics are important, both because it is the B/I unit that is typically managing the boundary with the corporate world and because the availability of other institutional options and approaches is a key ingredient of organizational adaptation to the environment (Cameron, 1984).

In the university, the closest parallel to a community college B/I unit would be what is often called an "Office of Contracted Services (or Sponsored Programs)," frequently modeled on (or congruent with) offices designed for interaction with the federal government for research grants. Such an office is responsible for promoting, brokering, and sometimes overseeing the administrative end of some research contracts with industry. Here, however, the parallel to the community college office ends, both because there are important differences in independence and autonomy between them and because the Office of Contracted Services (OCS) is only one of several structures that facilitate business- and industry-oriented activities at the university level.

OCS units have less autonomy in dealing with companies because at the university level a greater decision-making role is retained by individual faculty members and departments. The expertise for which companies come to the university resides more specifically in the individual faculty members than it normally does at the community college. Consequently, an OCS is necessarily less client-centered and more resource-based in dealing with companies, and it must be much more dependent on the wishes of the faculty in responding to company requests. The drafting or electronics instructor at XYZ Community College who prefers not to be involved with a B/I program can be more readily replaced by an outsider than can the molecular biology professor and researcher at ABC University.

Similarly, although decisions about what to do or not to do with a company can be made without any academic oversight at the community college (provided that a program is not offered for credit), such decisions are less clear at the university. Sometimes a level of departmental review will be required. In fact, in contrast to the primary gatekeeping role of the B/I unit at the community college, there is some evidence that the shoe is on the other foot at the university. Some faculty members view OCS-type liaison offices as ' superfluous and objectionable" (Stankiewicz,

1986, p. 52). University professors often possess the clout that their community college colleagues lack, and some of them also feel that B/I units are usurping and getting in the way of their connections with companies.

Another reason for the relative lack of independence and importance of the OCS is the office's involvement with only a small portion of the spectrum of corporate-university interaction. If the activities on the continuum referred to earlier (Zinser, 1985) are slightly regrouped, they can be divided into four broad categories: consulting, departmental, extradepartmental, and spinoff.

The most common activity is in fact the least regulated: faculty consultation. An estimated one-third of university faculty consult, with more than half of medical, engineering, and business school faculty members active in consulting. While there are also widespread (although, to my knowledge, uncounted) consulting relationships at the community college level, a greater significance may be assigned to these activities at the research university level because of the higher status involved. This pervasive activity is largely unmonitored. Many institutions have no reporting requirements for consulting, just the general stipulation that it not exceed one day a week. For instance, most of Harvard University's graduate schools have different reporting requirements. There are none at the law school. In arts and sciences, as in the medical school, a professor makes a voluntary report to the dean if he or she is worried about a potential conflict of interest, and there is a voluntary self-report for an unpublicized, internal listing at the Kennedy School of Government and the business school (Weissman, 1988).

The second major kind of activity occurs in the departments, and it includes what Zinser (1985) refers to as procurement (the buying of contracted services), linkage (bringing together departments and outsiders), and exchange (of money for patent rights or affiliate "windows.") All these activities involve the faculty members and the departments, and these are the areas in which a liaison office or an OCS is likely to play a role as a broker and/or administrator. In most situations, the OCS will not only be dealing with an individual faculty member but will also be seeking the approval of a department.

The third and fourth levels of activity represent a relatively smaller volume but are significant in terms of new relationships formed. In both cases, the university goes beyond attempts to broker with existing (departmental) resources and creates an extradepartmental organization to provide services to existing companies. Here, the facilitating structure, if any, will vary widely from university to university. Often these extradepartmental entities will have their own governance structures that are different from anything preexisting on campus. For example, the Whitehead Institute was founded at MIT amid considerable faculty concern that it would be sharing MIT's prestige, have coappointments of faculty members, and yet be accountable to its own board, primarily composed of outsiders ("MIT Agonizes . . . ," 1981). The fourth level of activity is the establishment of new spinoffs, specifically to develop new products. This goes well past the traditional brokering role to include the creation of companies. Here, the facilitating structure of an OCS is even further afield. With the rare exception of a few universities that have set up programs for entrepreneurs, most of this comes about through the personal interest of the individuals involved. Even a university with an aggressive patent office interested in maximizing returns to the university finds that its faculty members frequently have their own webs of connection to industry through consulting relationships or previous commitments.

The contrast between the relatively tight, controlling, and autonomous managerial structure frequently seen in the community college and the more diffuse variety of facilitating structures at the university (with their greater regard for individual faculty members) sets the stage for the final section, on the management of boundaries between academia and industry. First, however, the following section examines the influence, actual and potential, that makes these boundary-management issues so vital.

Existing and Potential Influence

At the community college, the issues revolve around instruction—who should design, control, implement, and benefit from the instructional process. At the university, the issues have more to do with secrecy, conflict of interest, and the free and honest flow of research information. At the community college, the mechanism for influence is through the B/I unit; at the university, it is channeled through the faculty members themselves. There are important differences; yet, in both cases, powerful forces have been unleashed by the opening of the boundary with business and industry, which can have profound changes on these institutions of higher education.

At the community college, and most salient differences between the business- and industry-oriented programs and the rest of the college is the B/I units' outward, responsive focus and their hierarchical, "businesslike" organization. In contrast to the collegial use of faculty committees on the rest of the campus, in the B/I unit decisions are made by the director or by a staff member, and the decision maker generally extends more decision-making authority to the company than to the instructor. A recent how-to handbook is very explicit about the level of autonomy that colleges must be prepared to surrender in their interactions with companies:

Most college instructors, living beneath the umbrella of "academic freedom," are accustomed to prescribing for students information and methods of learning that they independently believe to be important. While this is appropriate behavior for the classroom, it will not be suitable for commerce and industry. Here we note, then, another major difference between your two worlds: in industry, industry controls! Industry will expect to influence the training content, the choice of instructor, the delivery method and the place and time of the activity, since industry will be paying the cost [Hamm and Tolle Burger, 1988, p. 14].

In addition to being more willing to yield decision-making authority to outsiders, B/I units tend to be leaner and more flexible than regular divisions. B/I directors pride themselves on offering whatever the company wants, whenever it wants it, starting immediately. Since they mostly use more inexpensive part-time faculty and run only courses for which there is a paying customer, B/I programs often produce revenue. The courses themselves tend to be more practical, less theoretical, and more focused on the needs of the companies than on those of students. Consequently, B/I units often develop approaches, structures, and attitudes toward institutional autonomy that look very different from those of the rest of the college.

Because so many B/I programs function in essential independence from their colleges, what frequently develops is a two-college system. As long as each remains in its own domain, any impact of B/I units on community colleges is minimal. The border between the college and the corporate world is theoretically open, but the boundary-spanning unit controls the customs gate and, in many cases, allows relatively little interaction between the company and the college proper.

There is evidence, however, that this situation of peaceful coexistence may not be very stable. Merely having a lean, responsive, revenue-generating wing, which is closely connected to powerful external forces, adds to the repertoire of what a community college knows how to do and can play an important role in organizational adaptation. Cameron (1984, p. 136) points out that educational institutions adapt best to their environments when subunits are strongly differentiated and display different cultures and attitudes toward their external environment. He argues that this "creative tension" will have "the effect of producing flexibility and adaptability, and it enables organizations to cope better with unpredictable environmental events." The impact becomes more noticeable in times of stress, when institutions are undergoing some sort of decline (perhaps in enrollments in their regular divisions). For instance, in the institution that Teitel (1988) refers to pseudonymously as Ellsberg Community College, the academic dean is quite consciously using the approaches and programs developed in the B/I unit to transform the college. The case is cited here, not as typical or even common, but as representative of a process that can be and is taking place, given the proper circumstances:

> Having started as a small component of a neglected, autonomous Continuing Education program in the 1970's, the B/I unit at Ellsberg has grown in recent years to exceed 40% of the full-time equivalent (FTE) enrollments and its presence is being significantly felt on campus. Because Ellsberg's state government reimburses B/I FTE's at a rate comparable to curriculum courses, and B/I operating costs are lower (1/3 the cost of producing a curriculum FTE), director John Conroy is regularly able to turn over $3 million of the college's $23 million budget. In the context of declining enrollments throughout the regular division of the college, this subsidy is not unnoticed at Ellsberg. It has been referred to so frequently in recent years that one senior faculty member is reported to have stood up at a departmental meeting and announced, "If I hear one more time how much money John Conroy is making the school, I'll . . ." [makes a motion to vomit].
>
> The B/I "approach"—which includes responsiveness to industry input in shaping courses, quick turnaround time on shorter-term courses, and even different work rules—is transforming the college. For instance, advisory committees have been revitalized for career programs, with a member of the B/I unit sitting in to make sure they are adequately (from the viewpoint of the administration and the B/I director) responding to the needs of the companies. New faculty hired in the technical division have 37 1/2 hour [per] week contracts, as opposed to the traditional 18 contact hours plus 5 office hours. The explicit understanding is that they are to be available to work for B/I as part of their load and will be evaluated and promoted accordingly. In tight fiscal times, regular faculty members interested in money for conferences or other development activities must turn to the B/I unit, which has the only discretionary funds around. But these monies come with clear strings attached: faculty members are expected to tie the conferences to increased business- and industry-oriented activities.
>
> The academic dean quite openly refers to B/I and Continuing Education as the research and development arms that will transform the campus into a market-driven, responsive, and up-to-date institution. For instance, as part of a B/I contract, a new office-automation program was developed, which featured the latest technology, competency-based instruction, and an open entry/open exit approach to teaching. When regular-division secretarial science faculty resisted implementing the approach, the dean set up a competing office-automation program on campus, through Continuing Education, using the part-timers employed in the B/I version until the older program folded and the faculty retired. The dean acknowl-

edges that the threat has been made quite explicitly: if you do not do it, B/I and Continuing Education will.

This transformation dynamic has led to a heightening of tensions and the presences of sharp "us/them" attitudes at Ellsberg. B/I staff see themselves as innovative, responsive, lean, and aggressive. They see many of the faculty members as conservative, complacent, out of date, and out of touch. (Not all the faculty is characterized this way: individuals sometimes earn praise as an exception, as in . . . "he [or she] has a B/I mentality.") On the other hand, many faculty members are shocked by the businesslike operation of the B/I office, by what they see as quotas on productivity and a scrambling for the dollar (or the FTE), without regard to quality or educational value. They are ultimately concerned about the impact this approach will have on the transformation of their college [Teitel, 1988, pp. 82–124].

While the Ellsberg case highlights the impact of business- and industry-oriented activities on a single school, a final approach to thinking about the overall influence of these activities on community colleges is to consider the subject from the perspective of the growth and evolution of the community college system. Many scholars see the relatively young community colleges as ripe for change. Deegan and Tillery (1985) divide the short history of community colleges into four generations and refer to the coming of the fifth-generation community college, without specifying what shape they think that institution will take. Others have already declared that a business and industry orientation should be a major (or the major) focus of the community college. For instance, Connor (1984, p. 29) declares emphatically and enthusiastically, "There is little doubt now that the introduction of industrial training into the two-year college environment will represent one . . . of the most historic events in all of higher education for the decade of the eighties." He argues that in serving employers work-force needs, the community colleges have found their niche. No longer will they be cast as junior or second-chance institutions, but rather as first-class technical training resources. Connor's position is supported by the authors of the American Association of Community and Junior Colleges' *1986 Training Inventory,* who view the partnership approach as the cutting edge of a metamorphosis in the community college system. Originally serving a preemployment population of eighteen- to twenty-four-year-olds, community colleges are now seen as increasingly meeting the "educational and training needs of working America." Furthermore, "given the population demographics and the technology-driven changes in the work force, there is good reason to predict that employee education and training could become the dominant force in two-year colleges" (Golattscheck, McKenney, and Mahoney, 1986, p. 71). Although it falls outside the scope of this chapter to argue the merits of this position, it is clear that the opening of the boundary to the corporate world also opens doors to influences that can have a dramatic role in reshaping community colleges.

The principal areas affected in the universities are research direction, secrecy, distortion, conflict of interest, and a fundamental challenge to departmental systems of reward and control.

When a committee of the American Association of University Professors prepared a report on corporate funding of academic research (Thomson and others, 1983), the first concern it addressed was the fear that corporate influence on research direction might move universities from pure research to applied research or product development. While this has been a persistent fear, a three-pronged counterargument has been advanced:

1. Industry will not push institutions to abandon pure research, since it is not in their interests.

2. A study of many consortia and research partnerships reveals that academicians are making most of the decisions about which research topics to pursue (Dimancescu and Botkin, 1986).

3. Someone with money is going to influence research direction. If it is not the companies, it will be the federal government; and why is corporate influence worse? Bok (1982) argues that industrial support often comes with fewer strings and less red tape than federal support.

Of greater concern is what has become a reign of secrecy. In fields and in an era where the flow of information is critical, as discoveries follow one another with breathtaking speed, any constraints on the flow of information are serious. The fear was formally expressed at a summit meeting for university presidents, scientists, and corporate personnel that corporate influence could "promote a secrecy that will harm the progress of science" (Bach and Thornton, 1983, p. 26).

Most research agreements address the corporate need to develop patents and protect proprietary information by giving companies prepublication review rights and a ninety-day delay in dissemination. This is generally argued to be a reasonable compromise that does not significantly slow down the flow of information. Unfortunately, there is evidence that the climate of secrecy just mentioned has affected many academic research labs. A scholar who clearly approves of and recommends the furthering of university-industry collaboration notes, "Even a single industrially sponsored R & D project, if it is large enough, may seriously affect the intellectual and social atmosphere of a department" (Stankiewicz, 1986, pp. 50–51).

The secrecy demands of corporate sponsors are not the only operating factors; some observers also note a "breakdown in normal familiar understandings governing the informal exchange of information and materials among academic scientists. It is widely reported, in fact, that academic scientists are now withholding information and materials with a view to making a private profit from them" (Thomson and others, 1983, p. 21a). Where once researchers strove for tenure and the Nobel Prize, now the possibility of personally making a few million dollars enters into the picture. The combination of factors can be devastating to the free and open flow of information. According to one research scientist at a major pharmaceutical company who has close ties to the academic community, "The situation has become reversed. It used to be that academic science was open and that everything at the companies was proprietary. Now I can call up my competitors and get more candid information, off the record, on what they are doing than I can get from my acquaintances in academic labs." He goes on to cite an example that summarizes changes in secrecy and communication, referring to an unpatented technique that became the basis of much modern biotechnology: "A major discovery of monoclonal antibodies was published quickly in the mid seventies. Everybody immediately started doing it; it became part of the public domain instantly. Today that would never happen. It would be patented first, published later, and people would have to buy licenses to use the process. There would be a definite slowdown."

Another change in the climate of academic science, driven by commercialization, is the likely increase in academic fraud or distortion for profit. These issues have been raised in the case of a research fellow at the Harvard-affiliated Massachusetts Eye and Ear Infirmary, who reportedly misrepresented his data and made more than a million dollars. In addition to using illegal procedures in testing a drug on human beings, he was accused of delaying the publication of the negative results of those tests, to prevent adverse impact on the price of stock he owned in a company that was planning to market the product (Gosselin, 1988). There is a long history of fraud in academic science, but until now the motive has been promotion, tenure, and academic fame. Commercialization adds a significant new inducement, which will undoubtedly emerge as an increasingly prevalent motive for fraud. Furthermore, abuses of the system may slip through: the traditional check on scientific misbehavior is the scrutiny of published articles, but some researchers may delay publication for business purposes. The case just mentioned also brings up broader conflict-of-interest issues. This researcher's supervisor was himself a stockholder in the company and personally gained $300,000 in sales of stock after the publication of the researcher's first article.

Aside from fraud and its potential, there remain the more general conflict-of-interest issues connected to serving both an academic and a corporate master. In the early 1980s, Harvard asked Walter Gilbert, a biologist and the founder of Biogen, to take a leave of absence to pursue his business interests, but that was rare and has become rarer (Gosselin, 1988). Harvard Watch, a Ralph Nader-inspired group of Harvard students, points to Harvard faculty members, like Myron Essex, who are actively pursuing careers simply fraught with conflicts on interests. Essex, who sits on the scientific advisory board of Cambridge Bioscience and owns substantial equity in the company, directs a lab at Harvard's School of Public Health that is sponsored by the company. When he recently patented an AIDS diagnostic drug, Harvard immediately granted an exclusive license to Cambridge Bioscience. The timing of the release of one of Essex's articles has been linked to the issuance of Cambridge Bioscience's stock (Weissman, 1988).

The final approach to examining the influence of corporate research is to look at it in the context of institutional change and the evolution of the university. Two types of potential change can be observed. The first type is structural and is related to the impact of these activities on tenure and rewards in academic departments. Several challenges to the departmental structure have been reported, centering primarily on the extradepartmental nature of many of the significant new collaborations. Dimancescu and Botkin (1986) conclude their look at R & D consortia by speculating that if a hundred consortia bloom, the corollary is that a hundred departmental barriers wither. They suggest that integration of disciplines is a key to solving modern complex problems, and that the power and relevance of the "intellectually entrenched departmental disciplines" should therefore decline (Dimancescu and Botkin, 1986, p. 133). In a more clearly articulated proposal, Stankiewicz (1986) calls for a new model of the university, in which disciplinary departments are augmented (not replaced) by nondisciplinary, technology-oriented units that could be better coordinated with the external interests of business and industry. Furthermore, he suggests a new career structure for academics, consistent with this broader outlook. A second and closely related change urged by Stankiewicz is the establishment or redirection of some universities toward technology, as opposed to classical science. An example of such a transformation is going on at Rensselaer Polytechnic Institute (RPI), Troy, New York, where even the architectural design of a new interdisciplinary technology center helps convey the message, as discussed by a college official (quoted in Dimancescu and Botkin, 1986, p. 107): "All the other RPI buildings are in buff brick color, reminiscent of the old American industrial era that was born in Troy. This new building is in high-tech white with bright red trim. More importantly, it physically integrates the ten different disciplines that work on the three centers by physically interweaving their laboratories with one another. We purposely disrupted life on campus by constructing a building right at the gateway. Everyone has to take notice of the new RPI. We are changing the culture of the established university." Is this an isolated case, or could such a transformation take place in other settings? Although the money involved in this case is relatively small as compared with overall research budgets,

Thomson and others (1983) note that the money is focused on relatively few universities and in relatively few academic areas.

As in the discussion of community colleges, the merits of these changes fall outside the purview of this chapter. Once again, the point is that the potential for this level of change exists as an outgrowth of the growing relationship with business and industry. Given these possibilities for influence, the final section of this chapter will explore the demands for proper oversight.

Implications for Responsible Boundary Management

The impacts and influences described in the previous section are not necessarily good or bad. Many are the natural consequences of opening up the boundary between two types of organizations. In fact, as suggested in the discussion of community colleges, what may be at work are appropriate evolutionary forces as organizations respond to changes in their environments. Nevertheless, if education institutions wish to be more than rudderless ships, subject to forces they do not understand and are powerless to influence, proper boundary-management structures need to be put in place. Some individual or group must be able to respond to a request from a business or industry and to draw the line thoughtfully, intelligently, and responsibly, saying, "We cannot do that and expect to remain the kind of institution we want to be" or "We will do this to meet the needs of the corporate sector and our own changing needs in relation to our environment, understanding full well the consequences for our own organization." The structures that we have seen already in place are not adequate to that task.

At community colleges, the key role is played by B/I directors. Not only do they represent the colleges, in the corporate world, they also often control information that reaches the colleges about possibilities on the corporate/collegiate frontier, and they have critical roles in determining what the college will and will not do. Like the boundary spanners described in Chapter One, they mediate between the worlds.

There are several conflicts inherent in this role. As sellers of services, B/I directors are often evaluated on how well they do this—quite literally, on the revenues they produce. Although B/I directors do not always have the final say about what their colleges will or will not do, they report to deans and presidents who may not be involved in the details of what these largely off-campus operations do. In times of fiscal austerity, there may be few incentives for a pressured president to say no to a lucrative deal.

Furthermore, boundary spanners, in general, often have weaker commitments to the core organization. Pressure to compromise with external norms brings ambiguity and divided loyalty, and this tension is exacerbated at the community college because the boundary-spanning role is often filled by a retired businessman or someone who has been chosen because of ties to the business sector.

Finally, a potential check on how institutions draw the line between what they will and will not do is frequently absent because, in most cases, the faculty members in colleges with independent B/I units have no oversight capacity. Since courses are noncredit and B/I staff can and do use outsider part-timers to teach them, there is often little or no interaction with the faculty.

The unusual case of one of the more integrated B/I units (referred to as Mountain Valley Community College in Teitel, 1988) gives some indication of how a disinterested faculty could play an important role in setting limits. At Mountain Valley, where the B/I unit uses full-time faculty in as many as 50 percent of its courses, one faculty member, who otherwise speaks very highly of the B/I unit and his involvement with it, describes an incident when a B/I staff member came in with a first-time request from a particular company for training in several skill areas. He and some colleagues drew up a proposal that was rejected because the company said it was too long. When the B/I staffer tried to exert pressure—or what the faculty members perceived as pressure—to run the program, the faculty had to "push back on the [B/I staff] to say it couldn't be done: 'We maintain a high academic standard and our integrity goes with it.' We were not going to do it. We understood that [the B/I staff] wanted a foothold into this company. But let's not tell them that we can do something that we can't" (Teitel, 1988, p. 56). The value of full-time faculty involvement in these programs was underscored by another interviewee at Mountain Valley: "Many administrators focus on part-time faculty because they are good, they are flexible, they provide no flak. They demand less curricular control [than full-time faculty]. Faculty members talk about excellence in education, and, with part-timers, administrators don't have to put up with that. But they may get lower quality. For instance, business and industry demands a specific training course. It takes someone with real grounding to resist that—to sort through the request and stand up and say, 'We cannot do that' " (Teitel, 1988, p. 81). But the Mountain Valley situation is unusual; by and large at the community college, faculty members are not active determiners of where the line should be drawn.

At the university, faculty are much more a part of the decision-making loop because of their relatively higher status and their indispensability to making the deal go. For instance, when MIT considered establishing the Whitehead Institute, a critical portion of the vote devolved to the faculty, especially to members of the biology department.

When high-stakes decisions like the one on the Whitehead Institute are made and individual faculty members become the bulwark, the pressures on those individuals must be evaluated. In addition to the pressures of departmental politics, what cannot be overlooked is the growing social norm of making money; faculty members may feel left out if they are not profiting from their research and investments. Although faculty members may become important deciders, they are also interested parties. For instance, the faculty members who would be seen as the bulwark against "going too far" at the Whitehead Institute have substantial investments of their own in biotechnology companies (Lepkowski, 1982).

Furthermore, the lines will be drawn differently in different places as institutions strive to keep their star professors. There was a take-it-or-lose-it quality to the Whitehead decision. An MIT historian who followed the incident with the Whitehead Institute sees the institute as potentially "lowering the standards of behavior in university after university. Biologists are selling themselves to the highest bidder and threatening to leave unless they can operate on their own professional terms. Universities that won't go along will lose faculty to places that are more lenient" (MIT historian Charles Weiner, quoted in Lepkowski, 1982, p. 11).

In addition to sometimes highly publicized decisions of whether to go along with particular projects, institutions must face the ongoing and less scrutinized day-to-day management of business- and industry-oriented activities. The case of the fraudulent researcher at Massachusetts Eye and Ear points to the weakness or virtual absence of a structure for supervision. Not only was his immediate supervisor a stockholder in the same company, but the lengthy and incomplete process of review undertaken by Harvard (only after complaints were brought to its attention) highlighted the institutional lack of a responsive and responsible structure. Harvard appeared reluctant to investigate the allegation, to censure the researchers, and to notify other institutions (where this researcher was then working) of its review, and Harvard appeared even more reluctant to address the issue in any public forum (Bourke, 1988).

In this chapter, I have developed the notion that increased activity across the corporate/collegiate border may have serious ramifications for institutions of higher education. Nevertheless, I have not recommended the maintenance of the status quo or suggested that these activities be curtailed to protect the sanctity of the ivory tower from the onslaught of crass businesspeople. On the contrary, I have stressed the importance of encouraging institutions of higher education to seek out opportunities in the external environment in a thoughtful and careful way. A strategic process needs to be developed that involves all segments of the academic community. It is a venture on which the future shape of the institutions quite literally depends; it is simply too important to be left to the boundary spanners alone.

Doing this properly is not an easy task and will call for all the strategic management advice that can be provided. Cross (1981, p. 6), in a farsighted article about the changing relationships between the academic and corporate sectors, writes that finding the right balance between on the one hand, relegating corporations to the status of "junior partners" and, on the other hand, selling the soul of the academy for a "mess of short-term benefits" is essential if colleges and universities wish to maintain a meaningful place for themselves among the new breed of educational providers. Lynton (1984, p. 88) also underscores the importance of business and industry for universities, and he challenges academics to devise a method of cooperation with business and industry "which imposes on academic institutions the difficulty of having to share authority without relinquishing responsibility."

As the 1980s come to a close, events have validated Lynton's and Cross's prophecies on the importance of academia's connection to business and industry. The challenge they laid out, years ago, of finding the proper balance between collaboration and integrity remains a challenge, a gauntlet still lying at the feet of the presidents, deans, directors, professors, and trustees of institutions of higher education.

References

American Association of State Colleges and Universities. *Exploring Common Ground: A Report on Business Academic Partnerships.* Washington, D.C.: American Association of State Colleges and Universities, 1988.

Bach, M., and Thornton, R. "Academic-Industrial Partnerships in Biomedical Research: Inevitability and Desirability." *Educational Record,* 1983, *64* (2), 26-32.

Bok, D. *Beyond the Ivory Tower.* Cambridge, Mass.: Harvard University Press, 1982.

Bourke, J. *The New Classified Research: Corporate Sponsored Biomedical Research and the Reign of Secrecy at Harvard University.* Cambridge: Harvard Watch, 1988.

Cameron, K. "Organizational Adaptation and Higher Education." *Journal of Higher Education,* 1984, *55* (2), 122-124.

Connor, W. A. "Providing Customized Job Training Through the Traditional Administrative Model." In R. J. Kopecek and R. G. Clarke (eds.), *Customized Job Training for Business and Industry.* New Directions for Community Colleges, no. 48. San Francisco: Jossey-Bass, 1984.

Cross, K. P. "New Frontiers for Higher Education: Business and the Professions." *Current Issues in Higher Education,* 1981, *3,* 1-7.

Deegan, W. L., and Tillery, D. "The Evolution of the Two-Year Colleges Through Four Generations." In W. L. Deegan, D. Tillery, and Associates, *Renewing the American Community College: Priorities and Strategies for Effective Leadership.* San Francisco: Jossey-Bass, 1985.

Dimancescu, D., and Botkin, J. *The New Alliance: America's R & D Consortia.* Cambridge, Mass.: Ballinger, 1986.

Eurich, N. *Corporate Classrooms.* Princeton, N.J.: Carnegie Foundation for the Advancement of Teaching, 1985.

Fox, H. L. "Can Academia Adapt to Biotechnology's Lure?" *Chemical and Engineering News,* Oct. 12, 1981, pp. 39-44.

Golattscheck, J., McKenney, J., and Mahoney, J. *Industry Training Inventory.* Washington, D.C.: American Association of Community and Junior Colleges, 1986.

Gosselin, P. "Flawed Study Helps Doctors Profit on Drug." *Boston Globe,* Oct. 19, 1988.

Hamm, R., and Tolle Burger, L. *Doing Business with Business: A Handbook for Colleges Planning to Serve Commerce and Industry.* Washington, D.C.: American Association of Community and Junior Colleges, 1988. (ED 300 088)

Jaschik, S. "Community College in Arizona Strives to Help Its Region's Economy." *Chronicle of Higher Education,* Apr. 2, 1986, p. 15.

Keep America Working Task Force. *Community College/Employer/Labor Partnership Awards.* Washington, D.C.: American Association of Community and Junior Colleges, 1986, 1987, 1988.

Kopecek, R. "Customized Job Training: Should Your Community College Be Involved?" In R. J. Kopecek and R. G. Clarke (eds.), *Customized Job Training for Business and Industry.* New Directions for Community Colleges, no. 48. San Francisco: Jossey-Bass, 1984.

Lepkowski, W. "Research Universities Face New Fiscal Realities." *Chemical and Engineering News,* November 23, 1981, pp. 23-32.

Lepkowski, W. "Academic Values Tested by MIT's New Center." *Chemical and Engineering News,* Mar. 15, 1982, pp. 7-12.

Lynton, E. A. *The Missing Connection Between Business and the Universities.* New York: ACE/Macmillan, 1984.

Lynton, E. A., and Elman, S. E. *New Priorities for the University: Meeting Society's Needs for Applied Knowledge and Competent Individuals.* San Francisco: Jossey-Bass, 1987.

"MIT Agonizes over Links with Research Unit." *Science,* Oct. 23, 1981, pp. 416-417.

National Governors' Association. "State Strategies to Train a Competent Work Force: The Emerging Role of State-Funded Job Training Programs." Paper presented to the National Governors' Association conference, Boston, Oct. 1986.

Shadows in the Sunbelt. Report on rural economic development prepared for the Ford Foundation, 1986.

Stankiewicz, D. *Academics and Entrepreneurs.* New York: St. Martin's Press, 1986.

Teitel, L. "The Impact of Business and Industry Oriented Programs on Community Colleges." Doctoral dissertation, Graduate School of Education, Harvard University, 1988.

Thomson, J., Dreben, B. S., Holtzman, E., and Kreiser, B. R. "Corporate Funding of Academic Research." *Academe,* 1983, *69* (6), 18a-23a.

Weissman, R. *Scholars, Inc.: Harvard Academics in Service of Industry and Government.* Cambridge, Mass.: Harvard Watch, 1988.

Zinser, E. "Potential Conflict-of-Interest Issues in Relationships Between Academia and Industry." In J. Bennett and J. Peltason (eds.), *Contemporary Issues in Higher Education.* New York: ACE/Macmillan, 1985.

Lee Teitel is professor of technology and departmental chair at Roxbury Community College. He is currently on leave and is a visiting assistant professor of educational administration at the University of Massachusetts, Boston.

The development of state higher education boards provides an example of how higher education institutions, as open systems, have had to select various strategies as a fundamental means of competing for scarce resources and survival.

Colleges and State Government: Problems or Opportunities?

Robert J. Barak

Colleges and universities throughout history have been profoundly affected by events outside academe. In fact, one could write a history demonstrating that all of the major changes in higher education have been the direct result of events taking place outside colleges and universities. Colleges have been basically open systems, demonstrating a fairly high degree of flexibility in adapting to their environments. This has occurred in spite of the "ivory tower" perception that many people have of colleges and universities. In effect, the institutions have accepted the notion that to survive they must adapt. Many feel, however, that this adaptation has a price—the slow dissolution of autonomy and academic freedom. This dissolution is perhaps most often expressed with respect to the relationship between colleges and universities and state boards of higher education. The remainder of this chapter will focus on the dynamics of this relationship.

Development of State Boards

Writing in the early 1970s about the development of coordination in higher education, Berdahl (1971, p. 28) notes that the "growth in numbers and types of colleges and universities and the richness of their offerings reflected the tremendous postwar growth in student numbers and led to huge increases in state expenditures on higher education." State expenditures, he noted, "rose from $500 million in 1950 to about $5 billion in 1967"—from 7 percent of state expenditures to about 15 percent. This growth and its accompanying complexities have resulted in higher education's becoming a major concern to state governments. Many states have met this challenge by the establishment of various kinds of boards to oversee this growth and development in higher education.

Berdahl (1971, p. 34) classifies the various state boards by the following categories:

- I. No board
- II. Voluntary boards
- IIIa. Coordinating boards with a majority of institutional members and with only advisory powers;
- IIIb. Coordinating boards with a majority of public members and advisory powers;
- IIIc. Coordinating boards with a majority of public members and regulatory powers; and
- IV. Consolidated governing boards with public members and responsibility for all of higher education or a significant segment thereof.

It should be noted that the classification of the various state boards is not an exact science. As Berdahl (1971, p. 24) has noted, the task of classification is complicated by at least three factors:

1. Board functions extend over a wide range of possible activities—planning, budget review, program approval, capital outlay review, administration of federal programs, to name only the major ones—and board powers may be advisory in some areas and regulatory in others.
2. There may be significant discrepancies between the de jure existence of powers and their de facto exercise.
3. The de facto exercise of powers may vary over time as the board confronts changing conditions in state government, higher education, or both.

Protective Strategies. Perceiving these boards, or even the prospect of such boards, as threats, the higher education community was generally opposed to their establishment. (Opposition varied, however, according to the degree of threat perceived, the particular environment in the state, and the nature of the issues—for example, some institutions saw competitive advantages in the proposed higher education boards.) The protective actions taken by the institutions ranged from occasional opposing testimony to outright campaigns involving institutional friends, alumni, and donors who were rallied into opposing forces. What happened as a result of this opposition was that the creation of the boards in some states was postponed a few years until some state crisis provided the ammunition to overcome the opposition. In other states, the boards were watered-down versions of originally proposed coordination.

Various kinds of avoidance mechanisms were used by colleges and universities, either individually or collectively, in an attempt to stop or contain these perceived intrusions on their autonomy. (Incidentally, it appears that the collective efforts were relatively more successful than the individual efforts.)

The first kind of avoidance approach includes attempts to convince those who are proposing coordination that colleges and universities are complex and therefore not well understood. In effect, the institutions' posture is that it would be best to leave them alone. This "equivocality" approach has traditionally been higher education's first line of defense.

A second strategy has been to play one sector of higher education off against another (for example, four-year institutions indicate that control is not needed for them but is needed for two-year institutions).

A third strategy, which has been especially effective in curbing coordination proposals and limiting coordination (if it is imposed), is to control information. This strategy includes providing only positive information, limiting the availability of data that could lead to effective oversight by a coordinating body, and providing untimely responses to data requests. Both the expense and the staff burden of providing requested data were used as reasons for not providing information.

A fourth strategy has to do with avoiding resource dependence. In some states, colleges have focused their avoidance efforts on limiting the coordinating groups' budget authority. To this day, some coordinating groups lack budget-recommendation authority or authority to develop consolidated budget requests (say, for all of postsecondary education) for action by the governor and the legislature.

Weakness of Early Boards. As a result of avoidance strategies aimed at attempts to impose increased coordination, many of the early coordinating boards were very weak. One approach, pursued in a few states, was the creation of voluntary coordinating boards, with institutional members, little or no staffing, and only the authority to do things mutually agreed to by the members. These boards gained impetus in the 1940s and 1950s but continued to develop in the 1960s, according to Pliner (1966).

The voluntary boards would probably fit into what Whetten (1981) has called the "mutual adjustment" form of coordination. This type of coordination is best characterized by its narrow set of common goals. The goal was often to do only what needed to be done to forestall the creation of the more threatening statutory boards. The aim, more positively stated, was to demonstrate that the state's colleges and universities could coordinate higher education on their own, without an imposed coordination structure and bureaucracy. Voluntary organizations also had many organizational problems that were frequently not overcome, such as issues regarding representation on the council, presidents and trustees, public versus private institutions, voting power, and so on (Allen, 1967).

The assumption behind voluntary boards was that self-coordination would be sufficient to demonstrate accountability on the part of higher education, without the threatening intrusion of persons from outside academe. The critical problem with these voluntary boards was that they generally failed the accountability test in the perception of those outside academe. They were often viewed as self-serving. The voluntary boards seldom took a hard look at higher education, rarely made definitive recommendations, avoided difficult decisions, and, perhaps most important, were not perceived by many as being objective. Some voluntary boards just did not sustain their initial enthusiasm for being alternatives to imposed coordination. Lacking credibility, these voluntary boards soon gave way to statutory boards.

The strong influence of the institutions also profoundly affected the nature and scope of the early statutory boards, which proliferated in the 1960s. Most were relatively weak, in comparison with their current-day counterparts. In state after state, a common scenario took place. As a result of the successful protective strategies used by higher education, the first coordinating boards were weak. They included at least some institutional members and had only weak advisory powers. These boards were often largely controlled by the institutional representatives, whose intricate knowledge of higher education was unequaled among the public members. Once again, the public members were frequently told how complex the institutions were, and that attempts at change or greater institutional compliance were therefore inappropriate or otherwise undesirable. These early statutory boards were also limited in their impact on higher education because they were able only to advise other groups (for example, individual institutional governing boards legislators). These weak coordinating boards largely represent what Whetten (1981) calls the "alliance" coordinating structure. They provided the linkage of an autonomous organization without the authority of a formal hierarchy. They could identify a problem or issue but had no formal authority to resolve it.

In many states, there was little interest on the part of the colleges and universities in seeing these early statutory coordinating boards succeed. Some institutional officials took the position that if the boards could be shown to be ineffective, their authority would be repealed, and the institutions could return to a more autonomous environment. Others worked hard to contain the authority of the boards, while a few tried to help the boards succeed. Each strategy had its successes and failures in the various states.

Many of these advisory boards ran into problems because they were found to be ineffective in addressing some of the issues identified by governors and legislators. Therefore, alternative coordinating mechanisms were sought. The advisory boards were often seen as lacking the influence to accomplish certain actions, such as implementing state plans for higher education and making effective budget and programmatic recommendations. These boards also frequently had small, weak staffs, and the level and quality of work were open to much institutional criticism (some justified). This problem was partly a reflection of the difficulty of attracting competent staff to the coordinating boards, because of uncompetitive salaries (especially vis-à-vis institutional salaries and benefits) and concerns about permanence of the new and often controversial coordinating boards (Glenny, Berdahl, Palola, and Paltridge, 1971). The new boards were, after all, "boundary" agencies between the governor, the legislature, and higher education institutions.

Staff work was also hampered in many states by the lack of any kind of state-level information system. By controlling information, the institutions were able to maintain fairly effective limitations on the activities of the advisory boards. Some also have felt that the majority membership held by the institutions exercised too great control over the actions of the advisory boards.

Strengthening of the Boards. Responding to these signs of ineffectiveness, and sometimes responding to new crises, states took action, beginning in the late 1960s and continuing today, to strengthen the coordination mechanisms by shifting majority membership from institutional representatives to public members or by eliminating institutional membership altogether, strengthening the staff in size and competence, increasing the regulatory responsibility of the boards (for example, developing budget and expanding program review and approval), and mandating information systems or otherwise facilitating their development. The 1970s were marked by maturation of the coordinating and governing arrangements of the 1960s (McGuinness, 1988). This maturation was further facilitated by the addition of responsibilities to the role of the coordinating boards.

First, the federal Education Amendments Act of 1972, under section 1202, prescribed that any state that desired to receive certain higher education funds had to establish or designate a state postsecondary commission for planning. Such commissions came to be known as the 1202 commissions. In response to this law, seventeen states established new commissions, nineteen designated existing commissions, and ten states augmented existing commissions (Millard, 1976).

Second, as state student aid programs were established in the 1970s and early 1980s, the state higher education boards were frequently given authority over those programs.

Third, concerns about "diploma mills" were addressed through the creation of state accreditation and licensure laws. Higher education boards in many states were given this added authority.

So frequent were the attempts to revise, augment, and strengthen the authority of the coordinating boards that several consultants even developed guidelines for states to use in restructuring and strengthening the coordination of higher education (Glenny, Berdahl, Palola, and Paltridge, 1971). Typical of the actions continuing this trend were changes in coordination in Colorado, Texas, and Washington, where the weaker boards were replaced by boards with more regulatory responsibilities. In Texas, for example, authority to set enrollment limits and strengthen planning was added in response to problems specifically identified by legislators.

In most states, these changes were evolutionary. They took place over time, usually in response to particular issues or problems when an existing board's authority was found wanting. Figure 1 shows the evolution of the state higher education boards since 1939. The long-term trend in state structures for higher education has been away from voluntary boards and the weaker, advisory coordinating boards, and toward stronger, regulatory coordinating boards and even consolidated governing boards. The latter have been more controversial because they have often resulted in the imposition of a new level of line administration between the governing board and institutional administrators. Millett (1984) notes that of the ten states in his study with statewide governing boards, seven had established the position of chief executive officer and three that of administrative officer without line authority. Indeed, consolidated governing boards, such as in North Carolina, often replaced individual institutional governing boards and were more strongly resisted by the institutions because the consolidated boards were less directly associated with the universities and were concerned with interinstitutional coordination, not just with the narrow needs of a single institution.

As a point of clarification, it should be noted that the consolidated governing boards are not new. Some date from the late 1800s. No state adopting this structure has ever abandoned it. Thus, these boards remain an alternative in state approaches to the organization of higher education. In the past ten years, consolidated governing boards have been considered in fifteen or more states (McGuinness, 1980); nevertheless, because of institutional opposition to added layers of bureaucracy and the loss of institution-specific governing boards and potential intrusion, only one state has adopted this form since 1980.

It should also be pointed out that consolidated governing boards do not represent the end-all of coordination types. Several authors (Glenny,

Figure 1. Number of States in Each Category of State Higher Education Boards

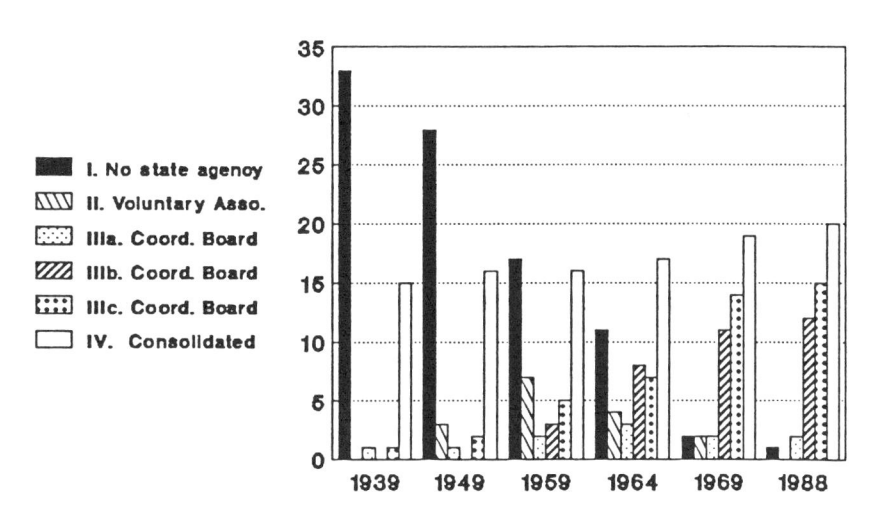

- I. No state agency
- II. Voluntary Asso.
- IIIa. Coord. Board
- IIIb. Coord. Board
- IIIc. Coord. Board
- IV. Consolidated

Source: Update based on Berdahl, 1971, p. 35.

Berdahl, Palola, and Paltridge, 1971; Millett, 1984) have indicated that the primary weakness of statewide governing boards is their general inadequacy as statewide planning and advisory agencies in higher education. Their focus is frequently too narrow, with primary emphasis on day-to-day operations of the institutions rather than on broader statewide concerns. Millett (1984) notes that among ten states identified in his study as having statewide governing boards, eight have established postsecondary planning commissions apart from the governing boards. For example, the dissatisfaction of the legislature with the planning efforts of the Florida Board of Regents, a consolidated governing board for the public universities in Florida, led to the establishment of the Postsecondary Education Planning Council (PEPC). The focus of PEPC is planning and coordination for all the postsecondary education in the state. Since 1984, at least one other state with a governing board has adopted a statewide planning agency. This, of course, adds yet another layer of coordination for colleges and universities.

No action with respect to statewide governance structures is ever final, as noted by an observer of the governance changes in Florida:

> The slippery and elusive nature of the concepts of "policy" versus "administration" and the tendency of a subgroup to regard establishment of "policy" by a higher authority as intervention in "administration" will provide the basis for some interesting maneuvering. It is likely that the

present calm may be a prelude to another attempt to solve the uneasy balance between universities seeking autonomy and those in both the legislative and executive branches of state government who wish to bring to the overall educational function rational planning and central direction of utilization of resources. The power now vested in the Commissioner gives some hint as to the shape of planning, governing and coordination, after the present Governor, who has an interest in education, is no longer in office. During the last session of the Legislature, legislators were distraught by the number of university lobbyists who descended upon the Capitol. At one time during the 1981 session, one university was represented by seven administrators lobbying simultaneously. Some were unaware of the presence of the others and two members of that area's delegation who serve on the same committee were given conflicting information. The General Appropriations Act contained a provision that each university could be represented by only the president of the university or his designee. This symbolic prohibition is likely to play only a precautionary role. If a master plan results in serious university-legislative infighting and the universities continue to seek legislative blessing for major program expansion, both of which are likely, the Legislature may soon again be faced with bills which propose to answer problems by changing structure [Mautz, 1982, p. 20].

As evidenced by the description of the situation in Florida, the debate goes on over the role of statewide coordinating and governing boards versus institutional autonomy.

The strengthening of the coordinating mechanisms for higher education has been a long-term trend in higher education, beginning in the 1940s and 1950s and continuing to the present time, but not all states have consistently followed this pattern. Some states have fluctuated over the short term. In Maryland, for example, institutional membership was eliminated in the early history of coordination and was restored five years later. More recently, the Maryland board has been replaced with yet another, much stronger, board. All members are public, and the board has stronger regulatory responsibilities. It is noteworthy that even this stronger Maryland board is weaker than the one originally proposed, as a result of institutional opposition and strong institutional lobbying efforts.

The net effect of the states' desire for greater coordination of higher education has been summarized as follows: "Coordination, regulation, and consolidation of higher education have been increasing rapidly at the state level. The free-standing campus, uncoordinated and unregulated and unconsolidated with other institutions, once the standard model, is increasingly a rarity in the public sector of higher education" (Carnegie Foundation for the Advancement of Teaching, 1976, p. 85). There are notable exceptions to this pattern. In Michigan, the state's constitutional autonomy for the major universities has kept the coordinating board's impact and other possible intrusions on institutional autonomy at a minimum. In a very few (mostly small) states, coordination has been reduced or kept at bay. For example, Wyoming discontinued its coordinating board, and other states, such as Delaware, have maintained relatively weak boards. It is not clear whether these states' colleges and universities were more effective in avoiding stronger coordination or whether in these states coordination was considered less important.

Implications for Boundary Management

Chambers (1961) asks a question that remains largely unanswered: whether institutions of higher education are today any better (or any worse), or whether one statewide system is any better than another, as a result of coordination. Several attempts have been made to address this question, but none has been successful to date, nor have there been any evaluations of college and university efforts to manage boundaries with respect to the issue of statewide coordination.

Every state has addressed this issue in one way or another, consciously or unconsciously. Changes and modifications are made to state boards' responsibilities almost every year in some states. Most recently, McGuinness (1988) has reported a countertrend in statewide coordination, toward decentralization and deregulation. The options adopted by some states and under consideration in others include the following:

> Increasing recognition of the importance of institutional governing boards. Actions include: efforts to improve the quality of gubernatorial appointments to governing boards, encouraging greater participation of board members in training programs and increased delegation to boards of management responsibilities previously controlled by one or more state agencies. Also related to this are conscious efforts to establish conditions that are conducive to attracting, retaining and rewarding effective college and university presidents.

> Increasing financial management flexibility for institutions. The most extensive changes involve a significant reduction in the number of line items in the state budget and delegation of extensive authority to institutions for shifting funds among programs and accounts, for carry-over of funds at the end of the fiscal year and for retaining and investing institutional revenues. In other states, detailed procedural controls in areas such as purchasing and personnel previously handled by executive branch agencies have been delegated to institutions.

Promoting institutional renewal through a combination of decentralized governance and increased use of incentives (changes in the base funding systems as well as new competitive categorical grant programs). These and other changes reflect a growing awareness of the limitations of traditional state fiscal and regulatory controls and an interest in exploring new policy tools aimed at stimulating effective decentralized management and a creative, "bottom-up" renewal within higher education. Deliberate attempts are being made to balance two approaches. On the one hand, centralized improvements will be made in strategic planning and resolution of major policy coordination issues. On the other hand, institutional renewal will be promoted through decentralized management and increased use of incentives rather than traditional policy directives and regulations [McGuinness, 1988, pp. 9-10].

Several national efforts have been made to categorize various functions in higher education decision making according to governance types. One such effort was described by the American Association of State Colleges and Universities (1971) as the development and expansion of state higher education boards was under way. This effort is shown in Table 1, which depicts the levels of decision for various higher education functions. This differentiation of functional responsibility was an attempt to identify the appropriate roles for institutions, state government as a whole, coordinating boards, and governing boards. Unfortunately, attempts at such differentiation have not been universally accepted. Many decisions fall into a gray area, where no consensus exists. These controversial areas are the battleground for daily interaction between the institutions and state boards.

Conclusion

This chapter has attempted to demonstrate some of the boundary problems and opportunities experienced by colleges and universities with respect to one external element: state boards of higher education. It notes the attempts by colleges and universities to protect institutional autonomy by various avoidance techniques. These strategies have had at least some impact on the nature of the intruding organizations, at least in the short run.

The persistence of higher education issues has kept concerns about coordination high on state legislators' agendas. Issues have often been dealt with through changes in overall governance structure. While these changing structures have varied over the years, as proper balances were sought between autonomy and accountability, no one structure has proved best. Instead, each state has attempted to resolve this balance through incremental changes in coordinating patterns (often when the solutions to problems could have been found without governance changes).

Table 1. Levels of Decision for Higher Education Functions

Function	State Government	Coordination Element	Governance Element	Institution
System organizational structure	Establishes broad structural arrangements. Defines role of elements.	Develops detailed coordinating policies and procedures.	Develops detailed governing.	Participates in development of coordinating and governance.
Program allocation	Adopts broad general guidelines.	Assumes major recommending and decision-making responsibility, recognizing interests of governing element and institutions.	Approves on basis of coordinating-element recommendations and institutional capabilities and interests.	Develops and executes programs.
Budget development	Very broad policy. Appropriates funds.	Reviews and relates budget to entire state's needs and recommends in terms of priorities.	Approves budget request with respect to justifiable needs (for own institution).	Prepare budget request.
Fiscal policies	Broad regulations, relations with other state agencies.	Organizes broad policy guidelines.	Approves institutional recommendations that conform to state and coordinating-element broad regulations and guidelines.	Executes broad policies and develops internal policies.
Program content		Approves in terms of needs of state.	Approves mainly in terms of institutional capability.	Proposes, develops, and operates.
Personnel selection	Establishes broad policy.	Coordinates among elements within state policy.	Approves institutional policies and considers institutional recommendations within policies.	Participates in development of policy and executes selection.

Table 1. *(continued)*

	\multicolumn{4}{c}{Elements in the System}			
Function	State Government	Coordination Element	Governance Element	Institution
Planning	Expresses state interests and needs.	Articulates plans of institutions and governing elements. Executes necessary statewide plans.	Expresses governing element interests and concerns. Coordinates with other elements.	Maintains continuous planning program. Initiates planning of institutional program.
Evaluation-accountability	Establishes basic requirements.	Coordinates among elements.	Establishes basic policy.	Executes policy, accepts responsibility for effective performance.
Capital programs	Very broad policy. Appropriates funds.	Approves in terms of state priorities and needs.	Approves in terms of institutional goals and needs.	Prepares and proposes capital program and recommends priorities.

Source: Adapted from American Association of State Colleges and Universities, 1971.

Over time these structural changes have resulted in a movement away from voluntary coordination boards and toward regulatory coordination and consolidated governing boards, with a corresponding increase in centralization and regulation. The boundary between higher education institutions and state governments is more blurred than ever before. We need greater diligence in the protection of institution integrity, while at the same time we must seek new opportunities in an environment where coordination is vital.

References

Allen, H. S. "Voluntary Coordination of Higher Education in Colorado." Unpublished manuscript, Office of Institutional Research, University of Nebraska, 1967.

American Association of State Colleges and Universities. *Institutional Rights and Responsibilities.* Washington, D.C.: American Association of State Colleges and Universities, 1971.

Berdahl, R. O. *Statewide Coordination of Higher Education.* Washington, D.C.: American Council on Education, 1971.

Carnegie Foundation for the Advancement of Teaching. *The State and Higher Education.* San Francisco: Jossey-Bass, 1976.

Chambers, M. M. *Voluntary Statewide Coordination in Public Higher Education.* Ann Arbor: University of Michigan Press, 1961.

Glenny, L. A., Berdahl, R. O., Palola, E. G., and Paltridge, J. G. *Coordinating Higher Education for the '70s.* Berkeley: Center for Research and Development in Higher Education, University of California, 1971.

McGuinness, A. C., Jr. *State Postsecondary Education Handbook.* Denver, Colo.: Education Commission of the States, 1988.

Mautz, R. B. *The Power Game: Governance of Higher Education in Florida.* Tallahassee: Institute for Higher Education, Florida State University, 1982.

Millard, R. M. *State Boards of Higher Education.* Research Report no. 4. Washington, D.C.: American Association for Higher Education, 1976.

Millett, J. D. *Conflict in Higher Education: State Government Coordination Versus Institutional Independence.* San Francisco: Jossey-Bass, 1984.

Pliner, E. *Coordination and Planning.* Baton Rouge: Public Affairs Research Council of Louisiana, 1966.

Whetten, D. A. "Interorganizational Relations: A Review of the Field." *Journal of Higher Education*, 1981, 52 (1), 1-27.

Robert J. Barak is deputy executive secretary of the Iowa Board of Regents.

Colleges and universities are effective to varying degrees in managing the boundary relationships between institutions and their environments on terms that are favorable for continued survival, growth, and improvement.

Interinstitutional Comparisons for Decision Making

Robert H. Glover, Michael R. Mills

This chapter applies what we have learned about boundary spanning from organization theory and the literature of higher education to a practical case study of environmental scanning and decision support for strategic planning and financial management in a private, comprehensive university, the University of Hartford. It reviews briefly the concepts that link environmental scanning and institutional effectiveness to strategic planning and monitoring of institutional performance. It gives an overview of the institutional and environmental context at the University of Hartford that motivated a comparative study of enrollment and financial strength of major private competitors, using external data from national data bases. This is followed by a description of the decision support system that the university developed to analyze the institution's enrollment and financial strength relative to its competitors. Finally, there is a summary of findings resulting from the environmental scanning, research methods, and use of the decision support system.

Confronted with a complex, uncertain, and rapidly changing environment, decision makers in higher education are increasingly aware of the need to improve the quality of information available for strategic planning, environmental assessment, and monitoring of institutional performance (Keller, 1983; Cope, 1987; Lelong and Shirley, 1984; Lozier and

Althouse, 1983). The essence of strategic planning is a dynamic process of reaching and revising consensus among leaders, members, and constituents on institutional mission, goals, and strategies, on the basis of a careful assessment of opportunities, risks, constraints, and threats in the external environment, a realistic appraisal of internal strengths and weaknesses relative to competitors, and a thorough analysis of resources needed for institutional survival, growth, and improvement.

Higher education institutions are affected, as are all societal institutions, by changes taking place in the macroenvironment. Each institution's influence over the macroenvironment is relatively limited. Hence, decision makers are forced to anticipate and adapt to major shifts taking place in demographic, economic, political, technological, social, cultural, ecological, and other trends. Colleges and universities, however, are in varying degrees effective in managing the boundary relationships between the institution and its environment on terms that are favorable for continued survival, growth, and improvement. The structure and composition of an institution's task environment is determined by its governance control (that is, public, private, religious) and by the mission and domains (for example, teaching, research, public service, national, regional, undergraduate liberal arts, graduate law) to which it has staked its claim and by which it has established its legitimacy and credibility with constituent publics. An institution's task environment consists of federal, state, and local governments, professional accrediting agencies, public and private funding sources, students, parents, school systems, alumni, employers, graduate schools, vendors, contractors, and institutional competitors.

An institution is effective to the extent that it manages the boundary relations with each constituent group in its task environment to:
- Enhance its prestige and image
- Achieve a high level of institutional and professional autonomy in managing its own affairs
- Be selective in acquisition of essential resources (that is, students, faculty, facilities, and funds)
- Achieve efficiency to invest in future growth and improvement
- Gain flexibility to adapt to changing opportunities, needs, and demands
- Establish a reputation for distinctive competence, reliable performance, and quality of service
- Satisfy the goals of members and constituents
- Motivate cooperation and support of members and constituents
- Successfully place members and constituents among society's power elite on the basis of valued and visible social contributions
- Gain a relative advantage over other institutions in competing for scarce resources.

The interactions among these dimensions of institutional effectiveness are, of course, very high; success on one dimension is likely to increase chances of success along other dimensions of institutional effectiveness.

Institutional and Environmental Context

As a private comprehensive university that is tuition- and enrollment-dependent, the University of Hartford over the next several years faces the difficult task of balancing institutional prices, student aid policy, and pressures for higher faculty and staff salaries and benefits against several realities: declining numbers of high school graduates, increasing competition for students, increasing resistance to tuition increases, and rising institutional costs.

The major private research universities and selective liberal arts colleges, by virtue of their long history, prestige, and reputations for academic excellence, can charge higher prices, select only qualified students, attract resources from diverse sources, and achieve levels of affluence that permit payment of higher faculty salaries. But tuition- and enrollment-dependent private institutions face much greater risks in balancing institutional prices, enrollment size, and admission selectivity against many competing demands for funds and relatively limited income sources as they seek to raise faculty and staff salaries and benefits, increase student aid, and improve the quality of academic programs, facilities, and administrative services.

The environmental scanning, research study, and decision support system described in this case study were designed to accomplish two major purposes: to develop a method for selecting appropriate peer and aspiration groups that the university can use to assess its enrollment and financial strength relative to other institutional competitors, and to build a decision support system to simplify the process of applying data, statistics, and judgment to perform interinstitutional comparative studies.

In a comprehensive review of the literature of interinstitutional comparisons in higher education, Brinkman (1987) cited the growing interest in interinstitutional comparisons and expressed the belief, shared by many administrators and analysts, that such comparisons among institutions can be a valuable management tool to gain an understanding of an institution's strengths and weaknesses and its relative competitive position. Nevertheless, the selection of peer and aspiration groups and the analysis of comparative data are often complex and risky, and few administrators and analysts in higher education have the necessary background to conduct and interpret the results of interinstitutional comparison studies.

Much of the early work on interinstitutional comparisons was motivated by pressures for accountability from legislators and statewide coordinating boards who wanted to gain increased control over educational quality and costs in public institutions. Planners and institutional researchers who have participated in interinstitutional comparison studies at the public-system level or the state level have expressed concern about the politics, institutional control, and technical aspects of interinstitutional comparison studies (Teeter, 1983; McCoy, 1987).

Nevertheless, interest in interinstitutional comparison studies continues to grow. The number of primary and secondary sources of interinstitutional comparison data is increasing, and applications and methods for comparative analysis are improving, notwithstanding known limitations regarding the timeliness and comparability of data and the lack of theoretical frameworks for the design of such studies (Christal and Wittstruck, 1987; Whitely and Stage, 1987).

As institutional uses of comparative data became more prevalent, the issue of how to select college or university peer and aspiration groups increased in importance. To address this need, a number of colleges and universities, both public and private, have engaged in voluntary data-sharing consortia to reduce the redundancy of effort in responding to requests for information, produce greater cross-institutional uniformity of data categories and definition, reduce the risks and costs of major survey projects, and enhance the legitimacy of comparison studies, both on campus and externally (Dunn, 1987).

Teeter and Brinkman (1987) described a typology of procedures used to develop peer groups for interinstitutional analyses, ranging from formal statistical methods like cluster analysis to hybrid approaches, threshold approaches, and panel reviews. Panel reviews and threshold approaches rely on institutional classifications based on mission, governance, and enrollment size and on qualitative and subjective judgments about reputation and competitive standing. Statistical methods like cluster analysis are more objective but still require judgment in selecting samples of institutions, identifying the critical variables, and deciding where to set boundaries between groups of institutional cases, as arrayed in a cluster analysis.

Recent work provides a conceptual framework for strategic planning and financial self-assessment that improves on the resources available for designing interinstitutional comparison studies (Frances, Huxel, Meyerson, and Park, 1987; Gale and Finn, 1985; Dickmeyer and Hughes, 1987).

Conceptual Framework for Research Design

Figure 1 displays relationships among the major components of the comparative analysis research design and the variables and ratios in each component that contribute to enrollment and financial strength, which in turn influence an institution's ability to pay higher faculty salaries.

Figure 1. Comparative Analysis of Enrollment and Financial Strength of Private Institutions Granting Master's and Doctoral Degrees

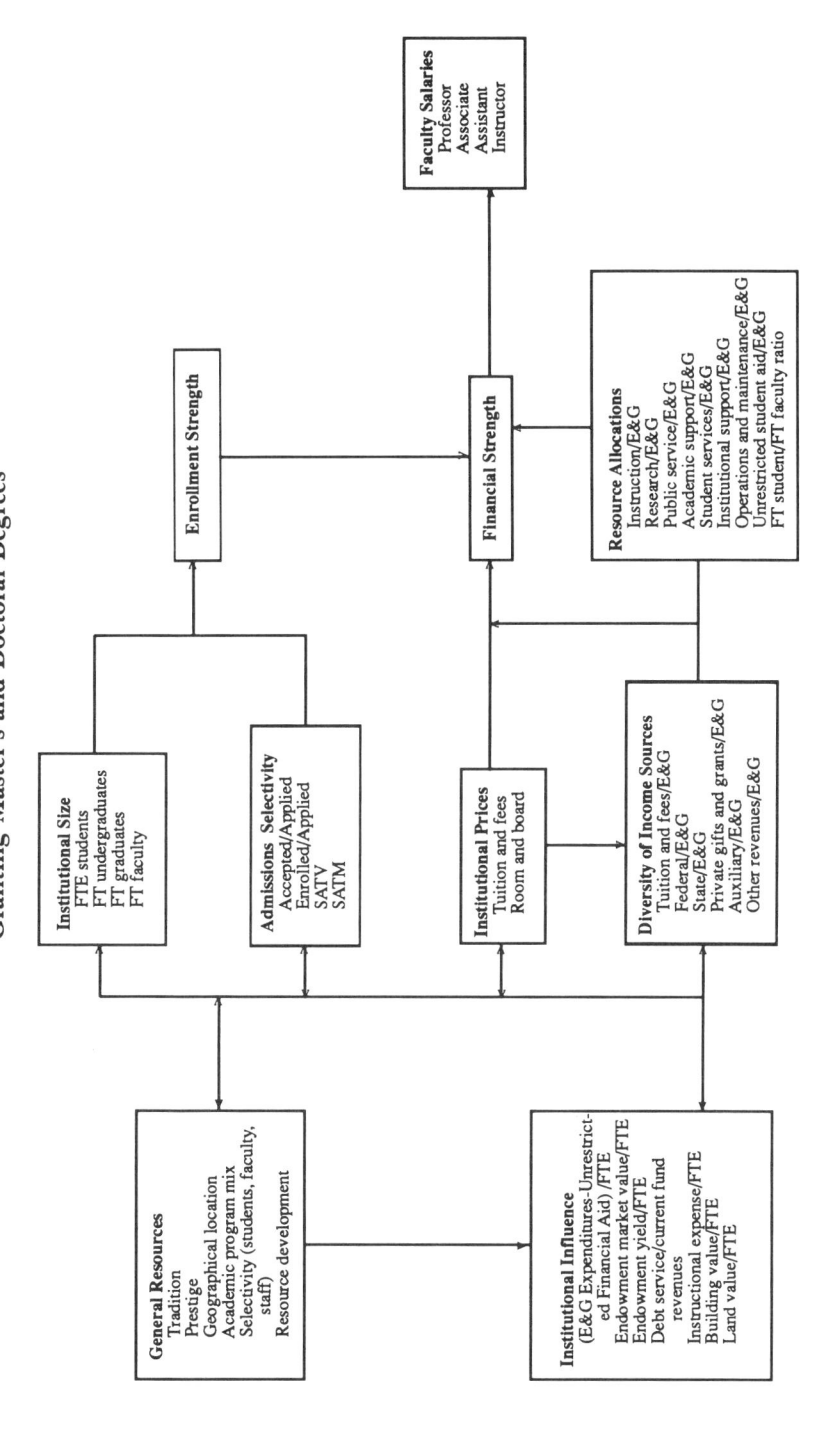

```
┌─────────────────┐
│ Faculty Salaries│
│   Professor     │
│   Associate     │
│   Assistant     │
│   Instructor    │
└─────────────────┘
         ▲
         │
┌─────────────────┐      ┌─────────────────────────────┐
│Enrollment       │      │ Resource Allocations        │
│Strength         │      │   Instruction/E&G           │
└─────────────────┘      │   Research/E&G              │
         │               │   Public service/E&G        │
         ▼               │   Academic support/E&G      │
┌─────────────────┐      │   Student services/E&G      │
│Financial        │◄─────│   Institutional support/E&G │
│Strength         │      │   Operations and            │
└─────────────────┘      │     maintenance/E&G         │
         ▲               │   Unrestricted student      │
         │               │     aid/E&G                 │
         │               │   FT student/FT faculty     │
         │               │     ratio                   │
         │               └─────────────────────────────┘
```

Institutional Size
- FTE students
- FT undergraduates
- FT graduates
- FT faculty

Admissions Selectivity
- Accepted/Applied
- Enrolled/Applied
- SATV
- SATM

Institutional Prices
- Tuition and fees
- Room and board

Diversity of Income Sources
- Tuition and fees/E&G
- Federal/E&G
- State/E&G
- Private gifts and grants/E&G
- Auxiliary/E&G
- Other revenues/E&G

General Resources
- Tradition
- Prestige
- Geographical location
- Academic program mix
- Selectivity (students, faculty, staff)
- Resource development

Institutional Influence
- (E&G Expenditures-Unrestricted Financial Aid)/FTE
- Endowment market value/FTE
- Endowment yield/FTE
- Debt service/current fund revenues
- Instructional expense/FTE
- Building value/FTE
- Land value/FTE

Enrollment strength depends on institutional size and admissions selectivity, as the joining lines and arrows in the model indicate. Institutional size—the number and mix of students relative to the size of the faculty—serves as one buffer against declining enrollments. The second buffer against enrollment decline is admissions selectivity, as measured by average SAT scores, the ratio of acceptances to applications, and the ratio of enrolled to accepted applicants (admissions yield).

Financial strength is most directly influenced by enrollment strength, institutional prices, and the extent to which an institution's educational and general revenues are diversified, rather than concentrated in tuition, fees, and auxiliary enterprise income, which are all primarily enrollment-driven. An institution's financial strength and its ability to pay higher faculty salaries are both contingent on the level, diversity, and flexibility of funding sources, especially income from endowments, annual giving, sponsored research, federal and state scholarship programs, and net revenue from ancillary enterprises.

Financial strength and funds available to pay higher faculty salaries are also a function of resource allocation, faculty and staff productivity, and efficiency of operations achieved through cost containment. The major issue is the balance of educational and general expenditures among mission-related activities (instruction, research, and public service) and support activities (academic support, student services, institutional support, and operations and maintenance). Other important resource-allocation issues must also be considered in the comparative analysis research design: faculty productivity (as measured by student-faculty ratios or credit hours per faculty member) and the extent to which student financial aid is funded with unrestricted operating funds (in effect, as a tuition discount), as opposed to endowment income or external funds.

Enrollment demand and faculty staffing, as measured by student-faculty ratios and students credit hours produced, are critical factors in the survival and financial strength of tuition- and enrollment-dependent institutions, especially of small private colleges with limited academic offerings. The major sponsored-research universities and selective liberal arts colleges are largely insulated from declining enrollment demand because their prestige and reputations for quality in academic programs and campus life attract many more qualified applicants than places in the entering class, because they can charge higher tuition and fees (that is, quality or status is perceived to be worth the high costs), and because they have abundant student aid to offer needy talented students. For sponsored-research universities and selective liberal arts colleges, threats to financial strength are more likely to be caused by economic downturns than by enrollment declines (for example, reductions in federal and corporate funding of sponsored research, failure of federal and state aid programs to keep pace with rising student costs, or failure of annual giving programs and endowment yields to keep pace with rising institutional costs).

Prestige and tradition are generalized resources that an institution can build only over an extended period of time, by establishing a reputation for distinctive competence through the quality of its academic programs and campus life. Institutional prestige and tradition are assessed qualitatively on the bases of the visible accomplishments of faculty, students, alumni, and staff and the loyalty that derives from their satisfaction as members and constituents. An institution's geographical location may be favorable or unfavorable for acquiring resources because of its sphere of influence (local, regional, national, international), its population density (urban, suburban, rural), demographic trends (growth, stability, decline) or economic conditions (economic growth, per capita income, employment rate). Having a mix of academic programs that are socially valued and in high demand enables an institution to be selective in choosing its students, faculty, and staff and in acquiring resources and funds on favorable terms.

Institutional affluence is a function of an institution's year of establishment, its ability to acquire resources, and its success in conserving resources to invest in future growth and development. Increasing affluence is necessary to increase the size, quality, and flexibility of an institution's endowment, land, buildings, and equipment, and to increase instructional resources relative to the size of its student body, faculty, and staff. Finally, the institution must maintain a favorable equity position, keeping its debt-service payments and current fund revenues in a favorable balance and weighing opportunities for growth and improvement against the requirement of prudent financial management.

Statistical Analysis and Decision Support System

Electronically encoded data from the 1985 HEGIS financial survey were obtained from Minter's Higher Education Data Service for all private institutions granting master's and doctoral degrees. Information on institutional prices, admissions selectivity, and institutional size were gathered from the College Board's annual survey of colleges and universities. Faculty salary data were gathered from an American Association of University Professors' (AAUP) report on the economic status of the profession. The data were assembled and integrated in a Foxbase data base on an IBM AT personal computer, and standard enrollment and financial ratios were computed with the NACUBO financial self-assessment indicators.

For purposes of the analysis, private institutions granting master's and doctoral degrees were first selected as the appropriate institutional reference group for the university. A selection was then made on the basis of full-time-equivalent (FTE) enrollment size, placing all institutions with enrollments under three thousand in one group and all those with enrollments over three thousand in another group.

The University of Hartford comparison group was identified with a cluster analysis of enrollment and financial ratios of the over-three-thousand FTE enrollment group, using SPSS PC. Cluster analysis is a procedure that separates cases into mutually exclusive groups according to the values of each case on a set of specified variables. The procedure begins with placement of one case in a separate group. It then creates another group by separating the remaining cases and continues to separate groups until each case is in a group of its own. While the procedure is separating new groups, it attempts to make each group as internally homogeneous and distinct from the other groups as possible, given the variables used.

For this cluster analysis, the data base included all private, comprehensive institutions and research universities in the United States with FTE enrollment between three thousand and ten thousand, augmented by a list of institutions that the university had used for interinstitutional comparisons in the past. Points in the cluster-analysis array were selected where the group separations created a reasonable size group that included the university. To test the validity of that group distinction and to see which variables distinguished those institutions from the others used in the cluster analysis, we ran a discriminant analysis, also using SPSS PC.

Discriminant analysis works in the opposite way from cluster analysis. It takes already identified groups and determines which variables make the groups different and assesses how accurately those variables can predict group membership. According to the discriminant analysis, the variables most useful for distinguishing the University of Hartford comparison group from the rest of the institutions were (in descending order) tuition and fee income, applied-to-accepted ratio, endowment income, financial aid expenditures, institutional support expenditures, research expenditures, accepted-to-enrolled ratio, private gifts and grants revenue, and state support revenues. Clearly, variables that measure each institution's revenue dependence and margin of admissions selectivity are important elements that distinguish the University of Hartford comparison group from other colleges and universities.

Discriminant analysis then uses an equation, based on the identified variables, to predict group membership for each case and then checks the predicted group membership against the actual group classification for all cases. In this analysis, the procedure correctly assigned 96.5 percent of the institutions to their appropriate groups; thus, the cluster analysis produced two highly distinguishable groups of institutions, and the nine variables identified in the cluster analysis provide a high degree of accuracy in predicting the group to which an institution belongs.

Multiple linear regression was used to identify which variables predict average levels of faculty salaries, by academic rank, across all three groups of institutional cases. The analyses produced multiple correlations of .95 for professors, .87 for associate professors, .85 for assistant professors, and .91 for instructors. As expected, the faculty salaries were highly correlated with the enrollment and financial strength of the institutions included in the analysis.

Finally, a decision support system (DSS) was built to refine the analysis of interinstitutional comparisons on the basis of case-study reviews. The DSS is a user-friendly system of menus and screens, developed with Foxbase data-base software, that can be used with a data dictionary to analyze and prepare comparative reports from the institutional data base without the need to write a computer program. The DSS menu system enables the user to print a data dictionary that lists all variables, select records and data fields, rank institutions on a selected variable within a specified range and make a line-by-line comparison of all variables and enrollment-financial ratios for any two institutions. The comparison report parallels the organization of variables presented in Figure 1 and the data dictionary used in the system. The case-by-case comparisons are especially useful for identifying subtle differences among institutions in their relative enrollment and financial strength.

Comparisons Among Institutional Clusters

Having divided the sample of 221 private institutions into two groups based on enrollment size, cluster analysis was used to array the institutions in the three-thousand-and-above group on measures of enrollment and financial strength. Discriminant analysis was performed on the under-three-thousand institutions with the two groups of larger institutions created in the cluster analysis. The three institutional groups were about equally represented in the sample of 172 institutions with usable data. The three resulting institutional groups were clearly identifiable, by both name and statistical profile, as predominantly private research universities, private comprehensive universities, or small private colleges.

Private comprehensive universities, including the University of Hartford, has enrollments that were less than 50 percent of the enrollments of private research universities and nearly 300 percent of the average enrollments of the small private colleges.

Admissions selectivity (the ratio of acceptances to applications) was significantly higher (.55) at the private research universities relative to the other two groups (.72), but admissions yield (ratio of enrolled to accepted students) was very similar across groups (ranging from .42 to .46).

Institutional prices were significantly higher at the private research universities—about $2,100 higher for tuition and fees, and about $600 higher for room and board relative to the average prices for private comprehensive universities and small private colleges.

The ratio of tuition and fee income to educational and general (E&G) expense indicated a very concentrated dependence on tuition and fees at private comprehensive universities (.77) and small private colleges (.69). Auxiliary enterprise income, also driven by student enrollment and fees, represented a significant percentage (between .16 and .20) of the remaining income sources available to private comprehensive universities and small private colleges (except, of course, for institutions having large commuter populations).

Income to E&G expense ratios at private research universities revealed much more diversified pattern of income sources: tuition and fees (.48), federal gifts and grants (.20), and other revenues (.42). Federal gifts and grants and other revenues (from hospitals for example, and research centers) at private research universities were proportionately higher, about double the comparable ratios for the private comprehensive universities and the small private colleges.

On the basis of dollar values per full-time-equivalent student, private research universities were, on the average, between two and five times more affluent than small private colleges and private comprehensive universities, depending on the measure selected. Small private colleges were about 20 percent higher than private comprehensive universities on most of the selected affluence indicators. The variables, divided by FTE students to compute the dollar value per full-time-equivalent student, were endowment book value, building value, equipment value, E&G expense less unrestricted aid, instructional expense, and endowment yield.

Student-faculty ratios at private research universities (13.5:1) and at small private colleges (14:1) were also significantly lower than the corresponding ratios for private comprehensive universities (17.5:1).

The resource-allocation pattern among the three groups also reflected differences in mission focus and economies of scale. Overall, the three groups of institutions spent between .38 and .42 of their E&G expenditures on instruction, between .08 and .10 on academic support, between .09 and .11 on operations and maintenance, and between .06 and .08 on student aid. Private research universities, however, allocated .17 of their E&G expense to research, whereas only .01 and .02 was allocated to research expense in private comprehensive universities and small private colleges. From the resource-allocation ratios for institutional support and student services, it is clear that private research universities and private comprehensive universities, because of their larger size, have certain advantages in economy of scale over small private colleges.

As expected from the patterns for admissions selectivity, income diversity, affluence, and resource allocation, average faculty salaries were much higher at private research universities than at private comprehensive universities and small private colleges among private institutions offering master's and doctoral degrees. Average salaries for professors at private research universities were 18 percent higher than for professors at private comprehensive universities and 31 percent higher than for professors at small private colleges. The same pattern of difference in average faculty salaries among institutional groups is indicated for the other academic ranks (associate professor, assistant professor, instructor), except that the percentage differences were somewhat smaller. Average salaries for the other academic ranks were about 10 percent lower for private comprehensive universities and about 20 percent lower for small private colleges relative to average salaries for comparable academic ranks at private research universities.

Comparisons with University of Hartford Peer Group

On the basis of the cluster analysis, the University of Hartford and thirty-five other institutions were selected as the peer comparison group for assessing differences in enrollment and financial strength. The University of Hartford ranks below the medians for the peer comparison group on measures of admissions selectivity, ratio of acceptances to applications, ratio of enrolled to accepted students, and average SAT verbal and math scores. Hence, the university would have less flexibility to maintain its enrollment levels and standards of academic quality in the event of declining numbers of applicants.

The university's prices for tuition and fees were slightly above the average for the peer comparison group, but its charges for room and board ranked near the top of the group (about 20 percent higher than the peer group average). At that time, therefore, the university was more constrained than its peers in raising institutional prices to compensate for any income loss that might result from unanticipated declines in enrollment.

The University of Hartford's FTE enrollment was slightly above the median for the peer comparison group and was above average for full-time and part-time undergraduate enrollments and for part-time graduate enrollments. The university was below the average enrollment for the peer group for full-time graduate students. Generally, the larger the enrollment, and the greater the diversity of academic programs (assuming reasonable demand), the more flexibility the institution has to sustain its enrollment levels in periods of declining demand. Nevertheless, program diversity (through curriculum proliferation and enrollment declines) can result in less than optimal efficiency and quality in some academic programs, especially in a small university, and this risk is exacerbated during periods of enrollment decline.

The size of the full-time faculty at the university ranks in the top third of the peer comparison group, reflecting a wide program array and the lower student-faculty ratios required for instruction in some programs, including art, music, engineering, and electronic technology.

All of the institutions in the peer comparison group have a concentrated dependence on tuition and fees and auxiliary income as revenue sources. The average ratio of tuition and fee revenues to E&G expenditures is .79; for auxiliary enterprise income, the average ratio to E&G expense is .17 for the peer comparison group. The corresponding ratios for the University of Hartford are about 1 percent lower for tuition and fees and about 3 percent higher for auxiliary enterprise income. The university spent more on student financial aid from unrestricted funds (11.7 percent of E&G expense) than the average for the peer comparison group (8.0 percent of E&G expense).

Generally, the university spent a higher percentage of its E&G budget on mission-related activities than average for the peer group; proportionately 4 percent more for instruction, 1.7 percent more on research, and 1.0 percent more for public service. The university spent proportionately less than the peer group on academic support (4.6 percent less), student services (3.2 percent less), and institutional support (1.5 percent less).

On the average ratios of dollar value to FTE enrollment (the indicators of institutional affluence in Figure 1), the University of Hartford ranked higher than its peer group on instructional expense, equipment, and E&G expenditures but below the peer group averages for land, buildings, endowment value, and endowment yield.

In recent years, the University of Hartford's average faculty salaries, as a percentage of peer group averages, have ranged between 6.2 percent and 9.8 percent below the average for professors and between 4.0 percent and 8.1 percent below the average for associate professors and assistant professors. Through repeated analyses of enrollment, financial, and salary data for peer comparison groups, the university has gained a better understanding of its enrollment and financial strength and of the opportunities and limits it faces in its efforts to offer more competitive faculty salaries.

Summary and Conclusion

Strategic planning and effective management are essential to long-term institutional survival, growth, and improvement in a turbulent environment. For decision makers who occupy critical boundary-spanning roles, it is important to anticipate conditions and trends in the external environment that are likely to have a favorable or unfavorable impact on institutional performance and to devise strategies that capitalize on opportunities and buffer potentially adverse effects of contingencies, constraints, or uncertainty. The research design and decision support system described in this case study have proved useful as tools in the process of environmental scanning and comparative analysis of enrollment and financial strength of peer and aspiration groups for the University of Hartford. The conceptual framework used in the study is informed by the open-systems theory of organizations and by recent contributions to the literature of financial assessment in higher education.

The analysis uses data available electronically at low cost from national data bases and takes advantage of fourth-generation data bases and statistical-analysis software to convert interinstitutional comparative data into information that decision makers can understand. Gathering data for comparative analysis of institutions, of course, is only one dimension of the process of environmental scanning. Environmental scanning also includes institutional-image studies, accepted-applicant surveys, admissions market-analysis studies, prospect and applicant-yield studies, alumni and benefactor studies, monitoring of changes in higher education prices, and comparison of faculty and staff salaries and benefits with those at other institutions. Interinstitutional comparison studies that are based on open-systems theory and on a conceptual framework for assessing enrollment and financial strength are especially useful in helping institutional leaders and their constituents gain a better understanding of the institution's competitive position, its relative influence or dependence in managing boundary relationships, and the opportunities and limitations of environmental forces that impinge on strategic planning, management decisions, and institutional performance at any given time.

To understand boundary-spanning relationships between the institution and its environment over time, longitudinal as well as comparative studies must be performed. An institution's stage of growth and development and organizational effectiveness can rise or fall in response to changing environmental demands, a leadership succession, an internal crisis, a strategic choice, increased competition, rising costs, or fluctuations in resource acquisition. Ultimately, improvements in institutional effectiveness are a function of leadership—the ability to diagnose opportunities and problems and to motivate action in response to changing institutional needs. Hence, access to better information about the institution and its environment is essential for decision makers to make better-informed strategic choices during this critical and dynamic period in higher education.

References

Brinkman, P. T. "Effective Interinstitutional Comparisons." In P. T. Brinkman (ed.), *Conducting Interinstitutional Comparisons.* New Directions for Institutional Research, no. 53. San Francisco: Jossey-Bass, 1987.

Christal, M. E., and Wittstruck, J. R. "Sources of Comparative Data." In P. T. Brinkman (ed.), *Conducting Interinstitutional Comparisons.* New Directions for Institutional Research, no. 53. San Francisco: Jossey-Bass, 1987.

Cope, R. G. *Opportunity from Strength Clarified with Case Examples.* ASHE-ERIC Higher Education Report no. 8. Washington, D.C.: ASHE-ERIC, 1987.

Dickmeyer, N., and Hughes, K. S. *Financial Self-Assessment: A Workbook for Colleges and Universities.* Washington, D.C.: National Association of College and University Business Officers, 1987.

Dunn, J. A. "Setting Up a Data-Sharing Project." In P. T. Brinkman (ed.), *Conducting Interinstitutional Comparisons.* New Directions for Institutional Research, no. 53. San Francisco: Jossey-Bass, 1987.

Frances, C., Huxel, G., Meyerson, J., and Park, D. *Strategic Decision Making: Key Questions and Indicators for Trustees.* Washington, D.C.: Association of Governing Boards of Universities and Colleges, 1987.

Gale, R. L., and Finn, D. F. *Financial Responsibilities of Governing Boards.* Washington, D.C.: Association of Governing Boards of Universities and Colleges, 1985.

Keller, G. *Academic Strategy: The Management Revolution in American Higher Education,* Baltimore, Md.: Johns Hopkins University Press, 1983.

Lelong, D., and Shirley, R. "Planning: Identifying the Focal Points of Action." *Planning for Higher Education,* 1984, *12,* 1–7.

Lozier, G., and Althouse, P. "Developing Planning and Budgeting Strategies for Internal Recycling of Trends." *Research in Higher Education,* 1983, *18,* 237–250.

McCoy, M. "Interinstitutional Analysis at the State Level." In P. T. Brinkman (ed.), *Conducting Interinstitutional Comparisons.* New Directions for Institutional Research, no. 53. San Francisco: Jossey-Bass, 1987.

Teeter, D. J. "The Politics of Comparing Data with Other Institutions." In J. W. Firnberg and W. F. Lasher (eds.), *The Politics and Pragmatics of Institutional Research.* New Directions for Institutional Research, no. 38. San Francisco: Jossey-Bass, 1983.

Teeter, D. J., and Brinkman, P. T. "Peer Institutional Studies: Institutional Comparisons." In J. A. Muffo and G. W. McLaughlin (eds.), *A Primer on Institutional Research.* Tallahassee, Fla.: Association for Institutional Research, 1987.

Whitely, M. A., and Stage, F. K. "Institutional Uses of Comparative Data." In P. T. Brinkman (ed.), *Conducting Interinstitutional Comparisons.* New Directions for Institutional Research, no. 53. San Francisco: Jossey-Bass, 1987.

Robert H. Glover is director of planning and institutional research at the University of Hartford.

Michael R. Mills is assistant vice-president for academic administration at the University of Hartford.

Colleges and universities can span boundaries effectively only if they plan for communication, and yet this central activity is often oversimplified or regarded as unmanageable.

Communication Across the Boundaries

Robert D. Gratz, Philip J. Salem

In a previous monograph (Gratz and Salem, 1981), we explored communication within the boundaries of colleges and universities. We noted that such communication within institutions of higher education is typically improvised, rather than planned. This loose management of information within the organization often leads to a situation of simultaneous overload and underload. Some individuals are overwhelmed with information, while others suffer from information deprivation, and some have far more information than they need on certain topics but inadequate information on others. Other authors have also considered internal communication in colleges and universities (Bonus, 1984; Newfarmer, 1981).

In the chapter, our focus is external as we explore the boundary-spanning activities of colleges and universities and the role that communication plays in the effectiveness of those activities. Although some types of external communication are more carefully planned than others, the general state of external communication is also characterized by inadequate planning. Communication is frequently regarded as an unmanageable process, and the seeds of failure are sown.

Characteristics of Boundary Communication

Before beginning our analysis of communication, we want to note four important characteristics of communication in boundary spanning. First, it is increasingly difficult to identify a boundary for social resources. By *social resources,* we mean inputs and outputs that are not physical material and not directly observable—such resources as information, satisfaction, and commitment. In our technological age, the lack of information in a university is more the product of university resources and pervasive attitudes than of any presumed ability of a gatekeeper to prevent information from crossing a boundary. It is more realistic to analyze the boundary spanning of a university's subsystems—its administration—than it is to analyze the boundary spanning of a university.

Second, the place of faculty in any university analysis is not clear. As we noted earlier, universities are loosely structured systems (Gratz and Salem, 1981). These loosely structured systems do not directly control the primary functions of teaching, research, and service; rather, faculty act as contractors to the system, employing the university to provide ancillary services and manage definitions. One method of analysis regards faculty as part of the system. Another method regards the system as ending at a department chair's or program head's office. Although we tend to regard the latter analysis as more reflective of the actual activities of higher education systems, we recognize that others tend to view faculty as part of the system.

Third, the premises of this volume present a view of homeostatic systems adapting to their environment. We do not share this view, especially regarding higher education systems. In our view, systems not only persist but also grow; that is, systems tend to evolve into more complex systems. This does not mean that colleges and universities do not experience periods of retrenchment; they do. However, the thrust of the external communication of systems is to affect the environment, to use the environment to its advantage. Left unattended, systems tend to maximize, not to stabilize. Universities tend to become more ambitious and expansive.

Fourth, communication is a process of information exchange. Some problems of universities are not communication problems but merely information problems, exchange problems, or process problems. However, communication in one part of a system often affects information or exchange or process in another. Every problem is not a communication problem, but communication tends to affect all parts of the system.

Our analysis begins with the model of communication we presented earlier (Gratz and Salem, 1981). The first component of that model is a communicator. In this case, we refer to the communication between an organization and part of its environment. Our concern is with the extent to which communicators' role perceptions are likely to influence their task perceptions. For example, a project director may perceive a program evaluation differently if it comes from a representative of a funding source rather than from a representative of a student organization. Perceptions will color subsequent messages.

A second communication element is the message, symbolic behavior. Our concern in the present analysis is with bandwidth, permanence, and style of message. Spoken language presented in a face-to-face setting has the greatest bandwidth. It has the capacity to carry the most information, and the inclusion of many nonverbal as well as verbal elements has the potential for greater redundancy and less confusion. Other forms of messages have a low information-per-message-unit capacity and greater potential for misunderstandings. Some forms of messages, such as messages on paper, overcome some of these difficulties because they have greater permanence. The permanent messages may be stored and retrieved, and the more permanent messages have greater political implications than the oral ones do. The style of a message is most important to the relational aspects of communication. Even if initial roles and role perceptions are compatible and favorable, a message constructed in an inappropriate style will destroy the communicator's effectiveness.

When the boundaries between a college and a surrounding system are spanned, the relationships that occur can be characterized by three qualities: the cohesion or the degree of involvement of the communicators, the adaptability of the relationship between the communicators, and the premium of exchange defining the payoffs that communicators receive from the episode. Cohesiveness or inclusion varies along a continuum that ranges from disengaged through connected to enmeshed. Adaptability ranges from chaos through flexibility to rigidity. The premium of exchange involves the mix of intrinsic, extrinsic, and instrumental rewards. Outcomes from this dimension, typically described in terms of the communicators' satisfaction with the relationship, may vary from dissatisfied to unsatisfied to satisfied.

An episode is a pattern of interdependent messages with a discernible beginning and end. The creation of episodes is evidence that communication has occurred. Even if communicators, messages, and relationships are favorable, communicators may be unable to construct an episode.

The communicators may limit their message exchanges to formal documents, interviews, and planned telephone messages. These types of episodes do not provide a social presence. Individuals get the feeling that they are communicating with an institution, rather than with another person. Lowered social presence reduces the likelihood of elaborated episodes and may encourage early termination of an episode.

Communicators may play out their various messages in an unsynchronized fashion. For example, when responses are delayed beyond the normal expectations of participants, synchrony is threatened. Lowered synchronization limits the elaboration of an episode.

Episodes may also be threatened by lack of interactivity; that is, a participant may construct a message that is less relevant to the other's message than to the originator of the message. The conversation falls apart because messages becomes less dependent on previous messages than they are relevant to other concerns.

Boundary-Spanning Activities

As we analyze the various boundary-spanning activities, we will describe the typical communication that is a part of these activities. We will describe typical problems and solutions. At the end, we will answer several questions related to the communication across all these activities.

Representing. When college administrators think of how communication affects their institutions, they are likely to think first about representational activities. These activities are performed when an administrator serves as spokesperson, speaking on behalf of the college with the goal of shaping the behavior or the opinions of others. The lexicon of representation includes such terms as *image, public relations, news service, public information, publicity,* and so on. Representing is central to such college functions as building a reputation, providing information to those outside the system, and fund raising. Examples of representation range from catalogues to news releases to speeches to marketing campaigns.

One significant communication issue related to this activity involves the need to focus clearly on the relationship instead of on the message. Far too often, university administrators focus on the content of a message while disregarding the relationship toward which the message should be directed. For example, university catalogues may be formal documents written by academic administrators for other academic administrators. Instead, they should be regarded as representational devices, directed toward a relationship between an experienced and knowledgeable individual providing guidance and persons with much less experience and knowledge—namely, a population of high school and college students. The writing style and language level of the typical catalogue make it likely that the function of representing the university effectively will not be fulfilled.

Efforts to enhance the representation of colleges and universities often focus on college trustees (Fisher, 1980; Hamilton and Hartstein, 1985) or on the college president (Perkins, 1983; Boxx, 1985). Many others in central administration also regard representation as one of their key responsibilities. Most of the people who are charged with representation are employed in ancillary areas of the university rather than in the teaching and research functions.

However, many persons are perceived as representatives of the institution when they really have no such responsibility. Institutional statements regarding academic freedom are often accompanied by statements defining academic responsibility, one way of noting that faculty members may easily be perceived as college representatives. Nevertheless, the question of how to prevent those who are not formal representatives from being perceived as representatives when they span boundaries remains unresolved. Indeed, in a system as permeable as a college, preventing this perception may be impossible. An institution is probably better advised to concentrate on developing methods for providing other representations that are so comprehensive that occasional problems caused by unofficial representations are seen by those outside the system as aberrations.

Institutional efforts to develop relationships with such bodies as alumni association boards of directors are based, at least in part, on the assumption that these bodies can assist the college in representing itself more effectively. Colleges must carefully define the representation that they expect board members to provide. Criteria for selection of board members must reflect these representational needs.

In the last decade, many stories and articles addressed the issue of representing the institution, but most were guidebooks that described how to represent an institution effectively or commented on techniques for expanding coverage of the college (Rock, 1980; Arsove, 1980; Gardner, 1981; Smith, 1981; Litten and Brodigan, 1982; Richard, 1983; Jones, 1984; Watkins, 1984; Gehrung, Johnson, Petrizzo, and Stubler, 1986; Gilley and Ackerman, 1988). Published articles have focused on the importance of preparation and planning as keys to effectiveness. Evaluating the effectiveness of an institution's representation has received more limited attention, even though such methods as institutional image surveys are available for assessing effectiveness. One study evaluating the effectiveness of the university news service at the University of California, Berkeley, has also been reported in the literature (Hafner, 1980).

The two examples in Figure 1 involve typical functions in which representing the institution is a critical activity. These examples illustrate communication during the representational function.

As these examples show, representing is sometimes a broadly based activity, with a wide range of individuals involved. In other cases, however, it is a highly focused activity. Relational variations are present, although the messages and episodes are quite similar. This similarity suggests that typical communicators do not show enough sensitivity to relational differences in representational activities.

Scanning and Monitoring. Colleges and universities are making novel attempts to adapt to a rapidly changing environment. Contemporary

Figure 1. Boundary-Spanning Activity: Representing

Accreditation Reviews

Typical Communicators
Faculty, staff, and administrators involved in committees or interviews

Typical Messages
Creating accounts, descriptions, and assessments
Formal self-study reports
Speaking and writing

Typical Relationship
(Between Local Institution and Accrediting Agency)
Cohesion: moderately connected
Adaptability: some rigidity
Rewards: intrinsic and instrumental

Typical Episodes
Telephone conversations
Conferences and meetings
Documents
Meetings between institutional representatives and accreditors

Annual Fund Drive

Typical Communicators
President
Fund-drive director and steering committee
Alumni or friends of the institution
Other potential donors

Typical Messages
Creating impressions, showing needs, demonstrating successes
Formal descriptive information packages
Speaking and writing

Typical Relationship
(Between Local Institution and Potential or Prior Donors)
Cohesion: moderately connected
Adaptability: relatively flexible
Rewards: extrinsic and instrumental

Typical Episodes
Telephone conversations
Conferences and meetings
Printed materials and mailings
Meetings between institutional representatives and donors

institutions are likely to be engaged in strategic planning efforts far removed from the stereotype of the ivory tower. Keller (1983) identified four major forces and shifts that by the early 1980s had encouraged colleges and universities to adapt this management approach: the changing student clientele, the disintegrating college curriculum, the increase in competition within higher education, and the technological imperative. To be effective, institutional planning efforts must be based on a careful assessment of opportunities and constraints in the environment. This type of boundary-spanning activity is known as *scanning and monitoring*.

A college must define what is relevant in its environment, thereby determining what to monitor. This step involves identifying significant forces in the institution's environment and deciding how to track these critical features. The institution must then develop adequate systems for gathering the information it needs concerning the environment. Unless an institution develops methods for gathering information that defines the relationship between itself and that environment, inappropriate responses are likely. For example, if a university correctly diagnoses a need for expanded research in its environment, concludes that it could fill that gap by becoming a great research university, but incorrectly diagnoses the relationship between itself and an environment that is not prepared to accept that role for the university, a great deal of time and effort may be directed toward pursuit of an unattainable goal.

One key issue related to scanning and monitoring involves a college's ability to develop interpersonal networks that link into the environment and permit it to recognize opportunities and constraints. Such periodicals as the *Chronicle of Higher Education* have become standard resources for scanning and monitoring. However, this kind of national publication provides information that must frequently be supplemented by informal networks that add specificity and local nuances. Colleges must maintain these informal relationships for effective boundary spanning.

Examples of scanning and monitoring include the practice, in some major research universities, of establishing a Washington office or, in smaller universities, of employing consultants to monitor federal actions. These efforts are generally directed toward expanding the college's awareness of opportunities for grants and contracts. Other examples include institutional membership in organizations, such as the American Association of State Colleges and Universities, that provide regular information about environmental changes through newsletters.

One frequent method of scanning and monitoring is the establishment of advisory committees. These committees may be established by a school dean or by an academic department and have as their common theme the notion of bringing professionals to a campus for policy guidance, fund raising, and so on. However, as vehicles for scanning and monitoring, these committees represent expanded channels, with the capacity for processing messages of greater bandwidth and bringing multiple perspectives to bear on current issues. To fulfill this purpose, advisory committees must be broadly based, involving individuals who have a wide range of experience and vision.

The two examples in Figure 2 involve typical functions in which scanning and monitoring are critical. These examples illustrate communication during review of government proposals and definition of community expectations.

As these examples illustrate, scanning and monitoring take a wide variety of forms. The permeability of a college implies that anyone in the system can be a communicator involved in this activity. Messages, relationships, and episodes also vary widely, and institutions should not expect to control this activity effectively. More problematic than the question of control is the question of gathering and making effective use of the information that comes into the system. The scanning and monitoring that go on in most colleges bring far more information into the system than can be processed effectively, and an administrator should consider how to establish internal systems to improve the availability of this information for decision-making purposes.

Information Processing and Gatekeeping. Colleges and universities

Figure 2. Boundary-Spanning Activity: Scanning and Monitoring

Reviewing Government Proposals

Typical Communicators
Faculty, staff, and administrators involved in environmental assessment
Governmental agency representatives

Typical Messages
Creating accounts, descriptions, and assessments of policy drafts
Preparing comments on drafts
Creating internal memoranda
Speaking and writing

Typical Relationship
(Between Local Institution and Governmental Agencies)
Cohesion: relatively disengaged
Adaptability: some rigidity
Rewards: extrinsic and instrumental

Typical Episodes
Telephone conversations
Exchanged memoranda
Conferences and meetings
Documents

Defining Community Expectations

Typical Communicators
President and key administrators
Community leaders
Alumni or friends of the institution

Typical Messages
Expressing concern or congratulations
Acknowledging suggestions
Speaking and writing

Typical Relationship
(Between Local Institution and Community Leaders)
Cohesion: mildly connected
Adaptability: somewhat chaotic
Rewards: extrinsic and instrumental

Typical Episodes
Letters
Telephone conversations
Conferences and meetings
Meetings between institutional representatives and community leaders

are in the information business; information processing is the basic thing that they do. In the classroom, in journal articles, in consultant services that faculty members provide, colleges and universities are information machines. Yet when these institutions attempt to use the available information in their environments as the basis for action, the effectiveness of the system is questionable. Information processing and gatekeeping involve institutional efforts to interpret, translate, and filter knowledge of the environment. In this area, there is a particularly strong link between the quality of external communication processes and the quality of an institution's internal communication systems.

Many communication issues are related to information processing and gatekeeping, but two of the most critical are the timeliness of information that comes into the system and the potential for distortion of information as the boundaries are spanned. A problem of timeliness occurs when information is not provided at the time of its maximum value. Episodes lack synchrony, and their consequences are often unanticipated. For example, the state higher education authority may issue new guidelines for preparing and submitting new program proposals, but the local system for distributing those changes to deans and department chairs may fail to provide the information in a timely manner. This lag in dissemination may occur because the language and forms of the external system must be translated into the code of the college. Extra work may be caused by forcing a department, rather than the gatekeeper, to revise a proposal into the correct form. Furthermore, unless the department receives clear information about where the internal system has broken down, the blame for the error may erroneously be assigned to the external system. The department that has to revise a program submission may interpret an internal failure to provide timely information as another example of a problem with an external regulatory agency.

A college's efforts to implement a strategic planning process provide another example of the way a problem of timeliness may appear in a boundary-spanning activity. An institution may conduct a collegewide strategic planning process beginning with environmental assessment, progressing through development of unit plans at several levels, and resulting in a university plan. However, if the time that it takes to develop the plan is great, the early "futures assessment" is almost surely out-of-date by the time the university plan receives final approval.

Strategic planning and other similar processes are often coded in languages that are unfamiliar to neophytes. To be successful, planning activities should include an interactive process that recognizes problems of timeliness and identifies gatekeepers, who continually update environmental information and correct the environmental assessment as necessary. This step is essential if the institution intends to construct appropriate tactical responses.

The two examples in Figure 3 involve typical functions in which information processing and gatekeeping are critical. These examples illustrate communication during the processing of grant applications and the recruiting of new students.

The activities of information processing and gatekeeping in a college are usually particularized functions. Individuals tend to regard their responsibilities narrowly and confine their activities to the formal responsibilities of their jobs. Boundary-spanning activities frequently take place within relationships that are low in cohesion and somewhat rigid, and these characteristics increase the likelihood of distortion and problems of timeliness. College administrators should attempt to deal with distortion through the message-enhancement techniques suggested earlier and should deal with problems of timeliness by trying to match the internal system's capacity for information processing with the tasks attempted.

Transacting. Colleges and universities are human systems, and many of the raw materials that are needed as inputs are human resources. Faculty and staff must be hired, and students must be recruited. Similarly, most of the outputs that leave the system and are integrated into exter-

Figure 3. Boundary-Spanning Activity: Information Processing and Gatekeeping

Processing of Grant Applications

Typical Communicators
Faculty, staff, and administrators involved in grant activity
External funding-agency representatives

Typical Messages
RPFs, grant applications
Institutional guidelines
Speaking and writing

Typical Relationship
(Between Local Institution and Granting Agency)
Cohesion: relatively disengaged
Adaptability: somewhat rigid
Rewards: extrinsic and instrumental

Typical Episodes
Telephone conversations
Conferences and meetings
Documents
Meetings between institutional representatives and granting-agency representatives

Recruiting New Students

Typical Communicators
Enrollment-management directors
Financial aid officers
Housing officials
Potential students and their parents
High school and junior college counselors

Typical Messages
Creating impressions, describing programs, providing information
Speaking and writing

Typical Relationship
(Between Local Institution and Prospects)
Cohesion: relatively disengaged
Adaptability: relatively rigid
Rewards: extrinsic and instrumental

Typical Episodes
Printed materials and mailings
Telephone conversations
Meetings between institutional representatives and prospects
Applications and responses

nal systems are human: students graduate or leave and must be helped through this transition. Other, nonhuman, resources and products must also be processed by the system—supplies, library books, software, farm products, and so on. Acquiring inputs and disposing of outputs is the activity known as *transacting*, and here, too, communication plays a part. Many authors have discussed transacting in colleges and universities in the last decade, particularly in the areas of marketing (Cooper, 1980; Coffee and Miller, 1980; Gregory, 1981; Andrew and others, 1981; Gaffner, 1981; Keim and Keim, 1981; Campbell and Spiro, 1982; Caren, 1987), fund raising (Strahler, 1980; Nichols, 1980; Stephany, 1980; Perkins, 1981; Ashton, 1981), and student placement (Apostolidis and Gougeon, 1986).

One issue that must be addressed as part of transacting is the management of communication channels. As we noted earlier, a college is a highly permeable system; therefore, boundaries are often difficult to maintain, and effective use of the system's resources may require the establishment of internal rules. These rules appear to define procedures, but they also define relationships. Purchasing standards and guidelines exemplify this pattern. These rules are designed to improve the internal management of resources by setting standards for transacting with the environment. However, these rules define relationships with external units and are often seen by those within the system as unnecessarily restrictive and cumbersome.

One problem is the inappropriate generalization of rules. Input rules, such as those provided by a state legislature, may be generalized and come into conflict with output rules that help define appropriate performance standards. In one situation, the manager of a university farm and the university's comptroller had to negotiate a solution to a rule conflict. State and local rules required three bids before items could be purchased, but external rules called for buying and selling cattle in public auctions. Clearly, the conflict between input and output rules required intervention through human communication to make transaction possible.

Tension between state higher education coordinating boards and public institutions within a state frequently exists because institutional representatives regard the external agencies as intrusive and see no institutional benefits that result from the boards' actions. If this kind of rule conflict is to be avoided, a richer communication environment must be created between the systems. Some communicators must be helped to understand the reasons for the control or to see the benefits of the restrictions, while others must learn how to adapt external rules to unanticipated circumstances.

Another communication issue can result from inaccurate assumptions about relationships and inadequate information about other communicators. For example, if a college is troubled by its difficulty in attracting interviewers to the placement center, it may spend a great deal of money remodeling the placement center in an attempt to provide a more attractive environment. However, if the actual reason for interviewers' avoidance of the campus is inadequate parking or inadequate academic programs, then a remodeled center will not solve the problem. A more relationship-centered approach, leading to greater interactivity and enriched episodes, is called for in this situation. The two examples in Figure 4 involve typical functions in which transacting is a central activity. These examples illustrate communication during the purchasing of materials and during a capital campaign.

As the examples show, transacting is a boundary-spanning activity that takes place in very different contexts in a college. At one level, transacting involves the president and other senior officials as they seek the kinds of general resources that sustain the institution. Transacting in this situation includes prepared messages but is also characterized by highly improvised transactions that include considerable flexibility.

Transacting also includes many routine tasks of the college, as institutional representatives use the institution's resources to acquire the materials that are needed for day-to-day operations. Transaction in this

Figure 4. Boundary-Spanning Activity: Transacting

Purchasing Materials

Typical Communicators
Faculty, staff, and administrators needing supplies
Purchasing agents
External company representatives

Typical Messages
Establishing policies and methods
Internal and external guidelines
Speaking and writing

Typical Relationship
(Among Local Institution, Regulatory Agencies, and External Suppliers)
Cohesion: moderately connected
Adaptability: considerable rigidity
Rewards: extrinsic and instrumental

Typical Episodes
Telephone conversations
Bid and contract documents
Informational meetings between institutional representatives and suppliers

Capital Campaign

Typical Communicators
President and other senior officials
Fund-drive director and steering committee
Foundation representatives
Alumni or friends of the institution
Other potential donors

Typical Messages
Creating impressions, showing needs, demonstrating successes
Speaking and writing

Typical Relationship
(Between Local Institution and Potential or Prior Donors)
Cohesion: moderately connected
Adaptability: relatively flexible
Rewards: extrinsic and instrumental

Typical Episodes
Printed materials and mailings
Proposals
Telephone conversations
Conferences and meetings
Meetings between institutional representatives and donors

situation is much more structured and much less likely to be improvised. Although many of the episodes are similar in these two types of situations, the degree of spontaneity is usually very different. If an institution attempted to treat the first type of situation as a strictly planned communication activity, or the second type of situation as a strictly improvised activity, boundary spanning would probably not succeed.

Linking and Coordinating. As noted earlier, the notion of the university as an ivory tower separated from its surroundings seems foreign to contemporary higher education. Today's colleges are likely to be involved in a variety of collaborative efforts—with industry, communities, public schools, and public and private agencies of all shapes and sizes. The boundary-spanning function that addresses the interorganizational connections or constraints of all of these relationships is the function known as *linking and coordinating*. One topic, discussed in the literature, is related to efforts to resolve conflicts between national security issues and scholarly research efforts (Rosenbaum and others, 1983; Shattuck, 1985). Another involves the implementation of linkages via emerging technologies (Allen, 1986; Lawry, 1986), and a third concerns establishing links with external agencies, such as governmental agencies or corporations (Ciervo, 1982; Bernstein, 1985).

One communication question that should be considered when a linkage is established with another organization is how intense the college wants the relationship to be. In some cases, external forces may answer this question. For example, the members of a board of regents may define the institution's level of involvement for it. In many cases, though, institutional leaders must determine whether they want a casual or a serious relationship.

Another way to frame this issue is to ask whether the college is trying to develop a suprasystem that integrates the linked systems or whether it is merely trying to develop more effective links between two parallel systems. The answer to this question helps to identify the linking points, or liaisons, and to define who will be the communicators acting on behalf of the college. This process must often be followed by actions empowering those made responsible for the linkage and informing external representatives that these individuals have been empowered. The higher the degree of integration desired, the more likely it is that institutional leaders will be involved in spanning the boundaries.

Project directors for externally funded programmatic grants often find that a significant portion of their job involves establishing links outside the college. Individuals with expertise in particular academic disciplines but no particular experience or training in the role of liaison are called on to manage this interface. One common difficulty is the tendency for the subject matter expert to be project-centered, rather than relationship-centered, and to give the impression of being a missionary who brings religion to the heathen. In such relationships, there is a danger of making the college seem pompous, paternalistic, and condescending toward the external individual or system.

The College Board's Educational Equality Project's Models Program provides one example of the variety of forms collaborative projects can take. This set of eighteen collaborative models is dedicated to improving the quality of curricula and increasing access to postsecondary education for at-risk students in the public schools. Participating institutions involved in the various models include public and private colleges, minority and nonminority institutions, and business and industrial partners in urban, suburban, and rural settings. The collaborative models include plans for a single college working with one school district or several school districts, for community colleges and senior colleges working together, and for a statewide collaboration between a university system and a state public education authority. Clearly, there is no one form that colleges employ when they engage in the activity of linking and coordinating.

The two examples in Figure 5 involve typical functions in which

Figure 5. Boundary-Spanning Activity: Linking and Coordinating

Working with Local Schools

Typical Communicators
Faculty and administrators especially those interested in teacher education
School administrators and teachers

Typical Messages
Creating impressions, showing needs, explaining programs
Speaking and writing

Typical Relationship
(Between Local Institution and School System)
Cohesion: moderately connected
Adaptability: some flexibility
Rewards: extrinsic and instrumental

Typical Episodes
Telephone conversations
Conferences and meetings
Documents
Meetings between institutional representatives and public school representative

Promoting Industrial Development

Typical Communicators
President, faculty, and administrators in affected programs
Local and state government officials
Chamber of Commerce representatives
Potential industrial representatives

Typical Messages
Creating impressions, showing needs, demonstrating successes
Speaking and writing

Typical Relationship
(Among Local Institution, Governmental Agencies, and Industrial Clients)
Cohesion: moderately connected
Adaptability: relatively flexible
Rewards: extrinsic and instrumental

Typical Episodes
Printed materials and mailings
Telephone conversations
Conferences and meetings
Meetings between institutional representatives and donors

linking and coordinating are significant. These examples illustrate communication during work with local schools and during promotion of industrial development.

Most of our comments about scanning and monitoring also apply to linking and coordinating. The activity is spread throughout the system, and many individuals in the system become involved in this activity. Messages and episodes are generally similar, but relationships vary considerably according to the importance that participants assign to relationships and relational intensity. How each communicator perceives the social role of other communicators has a significant influence on the importance assigned to tasks related to linking and coordinating.

Protecting. The final activity that a college or university uses in spanning boundaries is a defensive one. A college frequently must deal with external threats to the system. When the college takes action to maintain some degree of control over its own activities or defend itself, it is engaged in *protecting* (see Figure 6). In one instance, for example, the presidents of nine community colleges responded to a statewide economic crisis by forming a consortium to pool their resources and mount an aggressive marketing campaign (Boatright and Lestarjette, 1988).

One communication issue that often becomes relevant in this situation involves building a relationship characterized by trust in spite of strong differences of perspective and opinion. The level of trust between communicators helps define the relationship's cohesiveness. Building and maintaining cohesive relationships between systems when one of the systems is threatened is a very difficult task.

Protecting can be a matter of increasing the amount or the quality of information that flows from the institution. If external individuals or systems have inadequate information about a college, disagreements about specific issues can result. Since the courts have become a common forum for dispute resolution, colleges increasingly adopt a defensive posture on such issues as catalogue language (Davenport, 1985). This activity amounts to defending institutional definitions and protecting them from challenges as they are interpreted across the boundaries. Colleges also attempt to improve their messages to protect themselves from other environmental threats. During a time of retrenchment, the University of Michigan developed a comprehensive program to inform and develop support

Figure 6. Boundary-Spanning Activity: Protecting

Dealing with Threatened Budget Cuts

Typical Communicators
President and key administrators
News service director
Legislators or other funding agencies
Media representatives
Alumni or friends of the institution

Typical Messages
Creating impressions, showing needs, demonstrating successes
Speaking and writing

Typical Relationship
(Between Local Institution and Funding Agencies)
Cohesion: moderately connected
Adaptability: relatively flexible
Rewards: extrinsic and instrumental

Typical Episodes
Telephone conversations
Conferences and meetings
Documents
Meetings between institutional representatives and funding-agency representatives

Managing Unfavorable Publicity

Typical Communicators
President
News service director
Media representatives
Alumni or friends of the institution

Typical Messages
Creating impressions, refuting charges, demonstrating successes
Interviews, press conferences, and news releases
Speaking and writing

Typical Relationship
(Between Local Institution and Media Representatives)
Cohesion: relatively disengaged
Adaptability: somewhat chaotic
Rewards: extrinsic and instrumental

Typical Episodes
Newspaper and broadcast stories
Printed materials and mailings
Telephone conversations
Conferences and meetings
Meetings between institutional representatives and press

for funding of higher education (Yoder and May, 1980). This kind of effort often includes attempts to expand the channels, providing the capacity to deal with messages of greater bandwidth.

Protecting can also be a matter of spanning boundaries to review internal subsystems and, when necessary, taking corrective actions. In these cases, protecting an institution may include elements of the representational function. When an institutional crisis erupts, boundary management includes defensive representation of the institution (Thor, 1982). For example, immediately after the final game of the World Series in 1986, a serious racial incident erupted at the University of Massachusetts, Amherst. The institution's response included an investigation that involved both internal and external representatives. At least part of the institution's response was directed toward protecting the system from further disruption by using the information that spanned the boundaries for internal changes.

The two examples in Figure 6 involve typical functions in which protecting is a critical activity. These examples illustrate communication during a period of threatened budget cuts and during management of unfavorable publicity.

When a college is involved in protecting, the president or other senior officials are very likely to be key communicators. Internal media advisers are generally consulted, and external media representatives are also frequently involved. Messages from the college often tend to be excessively positive, while messages from outside are excessively negative. Perceptions of the roles of communicators from external systems may be quite strong and very negative. As a result, questions of credibility and trust are central, and cohesion is generally quite low. Synchrony is difficult to maintain, and poorly timed messages are common. When colleges engage in protecting, the communication problems described earlier in this chapter are particularly likely, and the corrective suggestions made throughout this chapter are especially relevant.

Conclusion

Colleges and universities are loosely structured systems whose basic business is information. Colleges engage in boundary spanning very frequently, but when they think about this activity, they frequently focus on formal messages. Communicators in this situation give the impression of presenting themselves in rather formal roles, and their messages are characterized by a relatively narrow bandwidth. However, excessive focus on planned messages may be accompanied by inadequate attention to development of the episodes that contain the messages. Episodes lack social presence, and problems of synchrony and interactivity are common. The relationships that result tend to be low in cohesion and adaptability, with limited payoffs.

As colleges plan for more effective use of communication in boundary spanning, specific activities must be carefully evaluated. Colleges must identify the four communication elements we described earlier—communicators, messages, relationships, and episodes—and must carefully evaluate the various kinds of difficulties that can occur with each. Colleges must supplement their message planning with greater attention to the development of episodes. Although many of the communication episodes that occur during boundary spanning are spontaneous, they do not have to be unanticipated or unplanned. Colleges should take a broader view of external communication than they normally do, and they should recognize that communication problems and opportunities that occur are likely to affect all parts of the system.

References

Allen, J. M. "Cable Television: Strategic Marketing Through Community Relationships." Paper presented to the annual convention of the California Association of Community Colleges, Anaheim, Nov. 1986.

Andrew, L. D., Shepherd, M., Lamb, S., Brandis, R., Griffin, E., White, E., and Fortune, J. "Marketing Higher Education in the Eighties." Paper presented to the annual meeting of the American Educational Research Association, Los Angeles, Apr. 1981.

Apostolidis, P., and Gougeon, D. "Positioning a University for Enhanced Student Placement." *Journal of Career Development*, 1986, *12* (3), 270-280.

Arsove, P. "Events Polish a Tarnished Image: A Case Study." *CASE Currents*, 1980, *6* (6), 30-31.

Ashton, R. R., Jr. "Pay-A-Caller: Employ Students to Staff Phonathons." *CASE Currents*, 1981, *7* (9), 14-15.

Bernstein, M. H. "Forging New Legislative Alliances: Higher Education in the State Capital." *Educational Record*, 1985, *66* (3), 30-31.

Boatright, J., and Lestarjette, S. "Houston-Area Community Colleges Reap Rewards of Cooperative Television Campaign." Paper presented to the National Council of Community Relations, Orlando, Fla., March 1988.

Bonus, T. (ed.). *Improving Internal Communication*. Washington, D.C.: Council for the Advancement and Support of Education, 1984.

Boxx, D. R. "Be Prepared." *Currents*, 1985, *11* (6), 28-30.

Campbell, J. F., and Spiro, L. M. "Evaluation of the Impact of Media Marketing Strategies on Continuing Education Enrollments." Paper presented to the annual forum of the Association for Institutional Research, Denver, May 1982.

Caren, W. L. "An Experimental Model for Market Penetration." *College and University*, 1987, *62* (2), 97-105.

Ciervo, A. V. "Catching the Legislative Eye: How Pennsylvania Colleges and Universities Developed an Editorial Support Campaign." *CASE Currents*, 1982, *8* (7), 40-41.

Coffee, L., and Miller, B. W. "Marketing Strategy for Community College Programs." *Community College Frontiers*, 1980, *8* (3), 10-12.

Cooper, E. M. "Guidelines for Presenting More Meaningful Information (in the College University Marketing Program)." Paper presented to the annual forum of the Association for Institutional Research, Atlanta, Apr. 1980.

Davenport, D. "The Catalog in the Courtroom: From Shield to Sword?" *Journal of College and University Law*, 1985, *12* (2), 201-226.

Fisher, J. L. "Trustees and the Media." *AGB Reports,* 1980, *22* (1), 26–30.
Gaffner, R. H. "Marketing and the Electronic Media." In W. A. Keim and M. C. Keim (eds.), *Marketing the Program.* New Directions for Community Colleges, no. 36. San Francisco: Jossey-Bass, 1981.
Gardner, G. "What Price PSAs? The Art of Adapting Your Information to the Needs of Broadcasters." *CASE Currents,* 1981, *7* (2), 38.
Gehrung, F., Johnson, J., Petrizzo, D. R., and Stubler, M. "How Can Community Colleges Work with the Media to Improve Their Public Image?" *Community, Junior, and Technical College Journal,* 1986, *57* (1), 32–35.
Gilley, J. W., and Ackerman, H. "How Strategic PR Can Pay Off." *AGB Reports,* 1988, *30* (3), 9–11.
Gratz, R. D., and Salem, P. J. *Organizational Communication and Higher Education.* AAHE-ERIC/Higher Education Research Report no. 10. Washington, D.C.: American Association for Higher Education, 1981.
Gregory, J. A. "Utilization of Marketing Techniques in California Community Colleges." Paper presented at the annual Community College Research Conference of the California Community and Junior College Association, March 1981.
Hafner, R. P., Jr. "Evaluate Your News Service." *CASE Currents,* 1980, *6* (1), 26–30.
Hamilton, J., and Hartstein, R. "Media and the Trustee." In G. F. Petty (ed.), *Active Trusteeship for a Changing Era.* New Directions for Community Colleges, no. 51. San Francisco: Jossey-Bass, 1985.
Jones, D. "Supplement Your Coverage." *Currents,* 1984, *10* (7), 40–42.
Keim, W. A., and Keim, M. C. (eds.). *Marketing the Program.* New Directions for Community Colleges, no. 36. San Francisco: Jossey-Bass, 1981.
Keller, G. *Academic Strategy: The Management Revolution in American Higher Education.* Baltimore, Md.: Johns Hopkins University Press, 1983.
Lawry, C. M. "The Effective Utilization of National Staff-Development Teleconferences: Recommendations from a Study of Users." Paper presented to the annual conference of the National Council of States on Inservice Education, Nashville, Nov. 1986.
Litten, L. H., and Brodigan, D. L. "On Being Heard in a Noisy World: Matching Messages and Media in College Marketing." *College and University,* '982, *57* (3), 242–264.
Newfarmer, T. D. "Let Your People Know: Good Employee Communication Means Good PR." *CASE Currents,* 1981, *7* (4), 32–33.
Nichols, S. G. "The Effective Use of Volunteers." In P. A. Welch (ed.), *Increasing Annual Giving.* New Directions for Institutional Advancement, no. 7. San Francisco: Jossey-Bass, 1980.
Perkins, D. R. "Getting Gifts Together: Alumni Media Experts Boost Capital Campaign." *CASE Currents,* 1981, *7* (6), 19–23.
Perkins, D. R. "Marketing Your Own Iacocca: How You Can Get Media Mileage for Your President." *CASE Currents,* 1983, *9* (8), 22–24.
Richard, G. T. "The Well-Bred Op-Ed: Increasing Your Institution's Exposure in the Press." *CASE Currents,* 1983, *9* (1), 32–34.
Rock, T. L. "Attracting Media Attention: Stunts Can Help, but Newsworthy Events Plus Good PR Planning Matter Most." *CASE Currents,* 1980, *6* (6), 36–37.
Rosenbaum, R. A., Tenzer, M. J., Unger, S. H., Van Alstyne, W., and Knight, J. "Government Censorship and Academic Freedom." *Academe,* 1983, *69* (6), 15a–17a.

Shattuck, J. "Harvard Report: Freedom of Scholars to Exchange Ideas Is 'Essential.' Text of 'Federal Restrictions on the Free Flow of Academic Information and Ideas.' " *Chronicle of Higher Education,* Jan. 9, 1985, pp. 13-17.

Smith, B.A.W. "Marketing and the Printed Media: Getting the Promotional Job Done." In W. A. Keim and M. C. Keim (eds.), *Marketing the Program.* New Directions for Community Colleges, no. 36. San Francisco: Jossey-Bass, 1981.

Stephany, R. J. "Phonathons: The Next-Best Thing to Being There." In P. A. Welch (ed.), *Increasing Annual Giving.* New Directions for Institutional Advancement, no. 7. San Francisco: Jossey-Bass, 1980.

Strahler, J. G. "Volunteers: Vital to the Annual Fund Campaign." In L. A. Maddalena (ed.), *Encouraging Voluntarism and Volunteers.* New Directions for Institutional Advancement, no. 9. San Francisco: Jossey-Bass, 1980.

Thor, L. "Effective Media Relations, or How Not to Make the Front Page." In P. S. Bryant and J. A. Johnson (eds.), *Advancing the Two-Year College.* New Directions for Institutional Advancement, no. 15. San Francisco: Jossey-Bass, 1982.

Watkins, B. T. "How to Get on the 6 O'Clock News, and Other Hints." *Chronicle of Higher Education,* Nov. 7, 1984, p. 26.

Yoder, S. L., and May, J. A. "Going Public: Michigan Awareness: A Program to Increase Public Understanding—And State Appropriations." *CASE Currents,* 1980, *6* (1), 18-20.

Robert D. Gratz is associate vice-president for academic affairs, dean of the university, and professor of speech communication, Southwest Texas State University.

Philip J. Salem is professor of speech communication, Southwest Texas State University.

Index

A

Ackerman, H., 97, 110
AIDS, 58-59
Aldrich, H., 10, 23
Allen, H. S., 68, 76
Allen, J. M., 104, 109
Althouse, P., 79-80, 92
American Association of Community and Junior Colleges, Keep America Working Task Force, 47, 64; *1986 Training Inventory*, 56
American Association of State Colleges and Universities, 46, 63, 74, 76, 99
American Association of University Professors (AAUP), 57, 85
American Council on Education, 29-30
American Demographics, 15
Andrew, L. D., 102, 109
Apostolidis, P., 102, 109
Arsove, P., 97, 109
Ashby, E., 26, 41
Ashton, R. R., Jr., 102, 109

B

Bach, M., 57, 63
Baden-Württemberg, 39
Barton, P., 34, 41
Benjamin Franklin Partnership Program, 40
Berdahl, R. O., 65-66, 69, 70-71, 76, 77
Bernstein, M. H., 104-105, 109
Betz, F., 38, 41
Biogen, and Harvard University, 58
Boatright, J., 106, 109
Bok, D., 17-18, 21, 23, 44-45, 57, 63
Bonus, T., 93, 109
Botkin, J., 37, 38, 41, 57, 59, 63
Boucher, W. I., 15, 24
Boundaries: described, 7-11; in higher education environments, 5-23; managing, 11-22; modifying, 22-23; properties of, 9-10
Boundary management: between colleges and communities, 60-63; between colleges and companies, 43-63; choices in, 40-41; and employers, 31-36; and state boards, 73-76
Boundary management activities, 11-22; linking and coordinating, 18-20; processing information and gatekeeping, 16-17; protecting, 20-2, 28; representing, 11-13, 28; scanning and monitoring, 13-16, 79-91; transacting, 17-18
Boundary spanning: case study, 79-91; and communication strategies, 93-109; defined, 9-10; representing, 96-97; three qualities of, 95
Boundary spanning activities: described, 96; linking and coordinating, 104-106; processing information and gatekeeping, 99-101, 102; protecting, 106-108; representing, 98; scanning and monitoring, 97-99, 100; transacting, 101-104
Bourke, J., 62, 63
Boxx, D. R., 96, 109
Brandis, R., 102, 109
Brinkman, P. T., 81, 82, 91, 92
Brodigan, D. L., 97, 110
Brown University, 20
Brown, W. B., 10, 23
Bruce, J. D., 35-36, 41
Business and industry (B/I) programs, 47-49; characteristics of, 49-53; examples of, 55-56, 61
Business-Higher Education Forum, 29-30

C

Cambridge Bioscience, 59
Cameron, K., 51, 54, 63
Campbell, J. F., 102, 109
Caren, W. L., 102, 109
Carnegie Foundation for the Advancement of Teaching, 72, 76

Chambers, M. M., 73, 76
Christal, M. E., 82, 92
Chronicle of Higher Education, 1, 3, 99
Ciervo, A. V., 104-105, 109
Cluster analysis, defined, 86
Coffee, L., 102, 109
College Board, 85, 105
Colleges and companies, 43-63; influence issues between, 53-60; new partnerships between, 44-46; new structures between, 49-53; research connections between, 48-49
Colleges, growth of, 26-28
Colorado, state boards in, 70
Communication model, 94-96
Communication strategies: for boundary spanning, 93-109; characteristics of, 94-96; defending, 106-108; information processing and, 99-101; relationship-centered, 104-106; and state boards, 103
Community college system, growth and evolution of, 56-57
Community colleges, customized job training in, 43-63
Competence, definition of, 30
Conference Board, 29, 41
Conflict of interest, 53-63
Connor, W. A., 56, 63
Containment, defined, 9
Contract training. *See* Job training, customized
Cooper, E. M., 102, 109
Cooperative Extension Service, 26
Cope, R. G., 79-80, 92
Corporate coordination, described, 19-21
Corwin, R. G., 9-10, 23
Cross, K. P., 62-63
Crosson, P., 40, 41
Cunninggim, M., 12, 23

D

Davenport, D., 107, 109
Decision support system (DSS), 87
Deegan, W. L., 56, 63
Delaware, state boards in, 73
Delta Community College (Michigan), and General Motors, 47
Des Moines Area College (Iowa), and Greyhound, 47

Dickmeyer, N., 82, 92
Dimancescu, D., 37, 38, 41, 57, 59, 63
Discriminant analysis, defined, 86
Dreben, B. S., 57-58, 59-60, 64
Dunn, J. A., 82, 92

E

Education Amendments Act of 1972, 69
Education and society, American history of, 25-26
Educational Equality Project's Models Program, 105
Educational patterns: alternative, 34-35; changes in traditional, 35-36; and maintaining competence, 33-34; from school to work, 31-33
El-Khawas, E., 19, 23
Elman, S. E., 20, 24, 40, 42, 50, 64
Emerson, R. W., 20
Enrollment and financial strength, of private institutions granting degrees, 83
Environmental information, interpreting, 16
Environmental pressures, responding to, 22-23
Environmental scanning, 79-91, 97-99
Environmental uncertainties, and organizational performance, 13-16, 18-23
Essex, M., 58-59
Etzioni, A., 7, 24
Eugenics, and University of California, 48
Eurich, N., 45, 63
Extended academic community, defined, 35-36
Exxon, and MIT, 19, 37

F

Fairweather, J. S., 38, 41
Fano, R. M., 35-36, 41
Ferguson, M. A., 12, 24
Finn, D. F., 82, 92
Fisher, J. L., 96, 109
Florida Board of Regents, 71-72
Fortune, J., 102, 109

Fox, H. L., 44, 63
Frances, C., 82, 92

G

Gaffner, R. H., 102, 109
Gale, R. L., 82, 92
Gardner, G., 97, 109
Gatekeeping, defined, 17
Gavert, R. V., 18, 24
Gehrung, F., 97, 110
General Motors, and Delta Community College, 47
Gilbert, W., 58
Gilley, J. W., 97, 110
Glenny, L. A., 69, 70-71, 77
Golattscheck, J., 46-47, 56-57, 64
Gosselin, P., 58, 64
Gougeon, D., 102, 109
Gratz, R. D., 93, 94-95, 110
Greenville Technical College (South Carolina), and Michelin, 47
Gregory, J. A., 102, 110
Greyhound, and Des Moines Area College, 47
Griffin, E., 102, 109

H

Hafner, R. P., Jr., 97, 110
Hamilton, J., 96, 110
Hamm, R., 53-54, 64
Hartstein, R., 96, 110
Harvard University, 44, 49; and Biogen, 58; Kennedy School of Government, 52; and Monsanto, 19, 20-21, 37; School of Public Health, 59
Harvard Watch, 58-59
Hatch Act, 26
Hearn, J. C., 15, 24
HEGIS financial survey, 85
Herker, D., 10, 23
Heydinger, R. B., 15, 22, 24
Higher education: business influences in, 53-63; consequences of growth in, 26-28; innovations in, 36-41; new patterns of, 31-36; openness and opportunity in, 25-41; and postindustrial society, 28-31; and state government, 65-76
Higher education environment, boundaries in, 5-23

Higher education functions, levels of decision for, 75-76
Holmes Group, 18-19, 24
Holtzman, E., 57-58, 59-60, 64
Huffman, J., 13, 24
Hughes, K. S., 82, 92
Huxel, G., 82, 92

I

Incubation centers, 49; described, 38
Interinstitutional data: analyzing, 85-87; and boundary spanning, 90-91; comparing clusters in, 87-89; and environmental context, 81-82; research design, 82-85; and University of Hartford, 89-91
Interorganizational connections, types of, 18-23

J

Jaschik, S., 47, 64
Jauch, L. R., 14, 24
Job training, customized, 53-63
Johnson, J., 97, 110
Jones, D., 97, 110

K

Keep America Working Task Force, 47, 64
Keim, M. C., 102, 110
Keim, W. A., 102, 110
Keller, G., 79-80, 92, 97-98, 110
Kennedy School of Government, 52
Knight, J., 104, 110
Kopecek, R., 46, 64
Kraft, K. L., 14, 24
Kreiser, B. R., 57-58, 59-60, 64

L

La Guardia Community Colleges, 35
Lamb, S., 102, 109
Lawry, C. M., 104, 110
Lelong, D., 79-80, 92
Lepkowski, W., 44, 62, 64
Lestarjette, S., 106, 109
Litten, L. H., 97, 110
Lozier, G., 79-80, 92
Lusterman, S., 34, 41

Lynton, E. A., 20, 24, 34, 40, 42, 50, 63, 64

M

McCoy, M., 82, 92
McGuinness, A. C., Jr., 69, 70, 73-74, 77
McKenney, J., 46-47, 56-57, 64
Mahoney, J., 46-47, 56-57, 64
Mann, H., 25-26, 42
Maricopa Community College system (Arizona), 47
Maryland Higher Education Commission, 19
Maryland, state boards in, 72
Massachusetts Eye and Ear Infirmary, and academic fraud, 58, 62
Massachusetts General Hospital-Hoechst agreement, 48
Massachusetts Institute of Technology (MIT), 45; Department of Electrical Engineering and Computer Science, 35-36; engineering curriculum at, 30; and Exxon, 19, 37; Whitehead Institute, 52-53, 61-62
Massachusetts State Board of Education, 25-26
Mautz, R. B., 71-72, 77
May, J. A., 107, 111
Meyerson, J., 82, 92
Michelin, and Greenville Technical College, 47
Michigan, state boards in, 73
Miles, R. H., 8, 11, 13-14, 24
Millard, R. M., 69, 77
Miller, B. W., 102, 109
Millett, J. D., 70-71, 77
Milliken, F. J., 16, 24
Minter's Higher Education Data Service, 85
"MIT Agonizes over Links with Research Unit," 53, 64
Monsanto, and Harvard University, 19, 20-21, 37
Morrill Act, 26
Morrison, J. L., 15, 24
Multiple linear regression, 86-87

N

NACUBO financial self-assessment indicators, 85
Nader, R., 58-59
National Clearinghouse for Teacher Assistant Training, 18
National Endowment for the Arts, 17
National Governors' Association, 47, 64
National Science Foundation, 17, 37, 48
National Task Force on Higher Education and the Public Interest, 12, 24
National Technological University, 33
Newfarmer, T. D., 93, 110
Newman, F., 20, 24
Nichols, S. G., 102, 110
Nobel Prize, 58
North Carolina: community colleges in, 45-46; state boards in, 70

O

Office of Contracted Services (OCS), 51
Open systems, colleges and universities as, 7, 91
OTTO, 40

P

Palola, E. G., 69, 70-71, 77
Paltridge, J. G., 69, 70-71, 77
Park, D., 82, 92
Parnell, D., 35, 42
Pennsylvania, Benjamin Franklin Partnership Program in, 40
Pennsylvania State Uviversity, PENNTAP at, 40
Perkins, D. R., 96, 102, 110
Perkins, J. A., 20, 24
Perkins Vocational Education Act, 35
Permeability, 97, 102; defined, 9
Petrizzo, D. R., 97, 110
Pfeffer, J., 8, 21, 24
Pliner, E., 67, 77
Portland Community College (Oregon), and Tektronix, 47
Postindustrial society, 28-31, 44-46; characteristics of, 29; and competence, 30; and critical thinking, 30
Postsecondary Education Planning Council (PEPC) (Florida), 71-72
Prospectors, defined, 14

Protective strategies, of colleges and universities, 21-22, 74

R

Renfro, W. L., 15, 24
Rensselaer Polytechnic Institute (RPI) (New York), 59
Representing institutions, who, what, and where of, 11-13
Research and development: collaboration in, 36-37; commercialization of, 37-38, 41, 48-49, 53-63; and technology transfer, 38-41
Resource-allocation pattern, 88-89
Rhode Island Partnership for Science and Technology, 20
Richard, G. T., 97, 110
Rio Salado Community College (Arizona), 47
Rock, T. L., 97, 110
Rosenbaum, R. A., 104, 110
Rowse, G. L., 17, 24

S

Salancik, G. R., 8, 21, 24
Salem, P. J., 93, 94-95, 110
SAT scores, 89; tracking, 15
Shadows in the Sunbelt, 46, 64
Shattuck, J., 104, 110
Shepherd, M., 102, 109
Shirley, R., 79-80, 92
Siebert, W. M., 35-36, 41
Smith, B.A.W., 97, 110
Smith-Lever Act, 26
Smullin, L. D., 35-36, 41
Social resources, defined, 94
South Carolina, community colleges in, 45-46
Spiro, L. M., 102, 109
Stage, F. K., 82, 92
Stanford University, 44, 45; Center for Biotechnology Research, 48; Center for Integrated Systems, 19, 37
Stankiewicz, D., 51-52, 57, 59, 64
State boards of education: and boundary management, 73-76; categories of, 66, 71; development of, 65-73; and interinstitutional data, 81-82; powers of, 19; protective measures against, 66-67; strengthening of, 69-73; and transaction standards, 103; weakness of early, 67-69
State government: and colleges, 65-76; and institutional autonomy, 20-22; and institutional growth, 27; and state advisory boards, 69
Stephany, R. J., 102, 111
Strahler, J. G., 102, 111
Strategic planning, and financial self-assessment, 82-91
Stubler, M., 97, 110
Syracuse University, Project Advance, 6-7, 18, 27

T

Task environment, described, 80-81
Technology transfer, 38-41, 45
Teeter, D. J., 82, 92
Teitel, L., 49, 54-56, 61, 64
Tektronix, and Portland Community College, 47
Tenzer, M. J., 104, 110
Texas, state boards in, 70
Thomas Edison Program (Ohio), and OTTO, 40
Thompson, J. D., 10, 14, 24
Thomson, J., 57-58, 59-60, 64
Thor, L., 107-108, 111
Thornton, R., 57, 63
Tillery, D., 56, 63
Tolle Burger, L., 53-54, 64
Transactions, defined, 17

U

Unger, S. H., 104, 110
Universities, growth of, 26-28
University of California (UC), and Eugenics, 48
University of California (UC), Santa Cruz, 5-7, 9
University of Hartford, case study at, 79-91
University of Michigan, 107
University of Pennsylvania, University City Science Center, 49
University of Rhode Island (URI), 20
University of Rochester, venture capital arm of, 48-49

V

Van Alstyne, W., 104, 110
Veysey, L., 26, 42
Vietnam War era, 45

W

Wall Street Journal, 15
Wallisch, B., 1, 3
Washington, state boards in, 70
Washington University, 44, 49
Watkins, B. T., 97, 111
Weiner, C., 62
Weissman, R., 52, 59, 64
West Germany, 39
Westinghouse Educational Foundation, 18
Whetten, D. A., 18, 19, 24, 67-68, 77
White, E., 102, 109
Whitehead Institute, 52-53, 61-62
Whitely, M. A., 82, 92
Wing, P., 17, 24
Wittstruck, J. R., 82, 92
World War II, 26, 28
Wyoming, state boards in, 73

Y

Yoder, S. L., 107, 111

Z

Zinser, E., 48, 52, 64

U.S. Postal Service
STATEMENT OF OWNERSHIP, MANAGEMENT AND CIRCULATION
Required by 39 U.S.C. 3685

1A. Title of Publication	1B. PUBLICATION NO.	2. Date of Filing
New Directions for Higher Education	9 9 0 - 8 8 0	10/27/89

3. Frequency of Issue	3A. No. of Issues Published Annually	3B. Annual Subscription Price
quarterly	4	$42 individual / $56 institutional

4. Complete Mailing Address of Known Office of Publication *(Street, City, County, State and ZIP+4 Code) (Not printers)*
350 Sansome Street, San Francisco, CA 94104-1310

5. Complete Mailing Address of the Headquarters of General Business Offices of the Publisher *(Not printer)*
(above address)

6. Full Names and Complete Mailing Address of Publisher, Editor, and Managing Editor *(This item MUST NOT be blank)*
Publisher *(Name and Complete Mailing Address)*
Jossey-Bass Inc., Publishers (above address)

Editor *(Name and Complete Mailing Address)*
Martin Kramer, 2807 Shasta Rd., Berkeley, CA 94708

Managing Editor *(Name and Complete Mailing Address)*
Steven Piersanti, President, Jossey-Bass Inc., Publishers (above address)

7. Owner *(If owned by a corporation, its name and address must be stated and also immediately thereunder the names and addresses of stockholders owning or holding 1 percent or more of total amount of stock. If not owned by a corporation, the names and addresses of the individual owners must be given. If owned by a partnership or other unincorporated firm, its name and address, as well as that of each individual must be given. If the publication is published by a nonprofit organization, its name and address must be stated.) (Item must be completed.)*

Full Name	Complete Mailing Address
Maxwell Communications Corp., plc	Headington Hill Hall, Oxford OX3 0BW, U.K.

8. Known Bondholders, Mortgagees, and Other Security Holders Owning or Holding 1 Percent or More of Total Amount of Bonds, Mortgages or Other Securities *(If there are none, so state)*

Full Name	Complete Mailing Address
none	

9. For Completion by Nonprofit Organizations Authorized To Mail at Special Rates *(DMM Section 423.12 only)*
The purpose, function, and nonprofit status of this organization and the exempt status for Federal income tax purposes *(Check one)*

☐ Has Not Changed During Preceding 12 Months ☐ Has Changed During Preceding 12 Months
(If changed, publisher must submit explanation of change with this statement.)

10. Extent and Nature of Circulation	Average No. Copies Each Issue During Preceding 12 Months	Actual No. Copies of Single Issue Published Nearest to Filing Date
A. Total No. Copies *(Net Press Run)*	2000	2085
B. Paid and/or Requested Circulation		
1. Sales through dealers and carriers, street vendors and counter sales	218	0
2. Mail Subscription *(Paid and/or requested)*	998	1086
C. Total Paid and/or Requested Circulation *(Sum of 10B1 and 10B2)*	1216	1086
D. Free Distribution by Mail, Carrier or Other Means Samples, Complimentary, and Other Free Copies	160	140
E. Total Distribution *(Sum of C and D)*	1376	1226
F. Copies Not Distributed		
1. Office use, left over, unaccounted, spoiled after printing	624	859
2. Return from News Agents		
G. TOTAL *(Sum of E, F1 and 2—should equal net press run shown in A)*	2000	2085

11. I certify that the statements made by me above are correct and complete

Signature and Title of Editor, Publisher, Business Manager, or Owner
[signature] Vice-President

PS Form 3526, Feb. 1989